BILL,
IT HAS BEEN AN
ABSOLUTE PLEASURE TO
WORK TO GETHER ON THE
2022 MUSKEGON PRAYER WALKS,
BUT MOSTLY TO CALL YOU FRIEND

DOUG

SIGNS
ALONG
THE WAY

Finding help and hope on the winding road of life
through the signs we encounter Along the Way.

BY DOUG MALEAR

xulon
PRESS

And the sign said "Long-haired freaky people need not apply"
So I tucked my hair up under my hat and I went in to ask him why
He said "You look like a fine upstanding young man,
I think you'll do"
So I took off my hat, I said "Imagine that.
Huh! Me workin' for you!"
Whoa-oh-oh
Sign, sign, everywhere a sign
Blockin' out the scenery, breakin' my mind
Do this, don't do that, can't you read the sign?

— Five Man Electric Band, 1971[1]

ENDORSEMENTS

When I first met Pastor Doug Malear, he told me his past and his plan to take root in the urban area in which I worked as a police officer at the time. I figured he might last a year at the most. Well, he is still there 20 years later and doing exactly what he told me he was going to do. Pastor Doug talks the talk because he has, and still is, walking the walk.

–Terry J. Sabo
Muskegon County Commissioner
Muskegon Heights Fire Fighter
Former Muskegon Heights Police Officer

God implants particular gifts within the lives of each of us. Doug has the special gift of taking spiritual truths and blessings and putting them into print. I am sure you will enjoy the truth, love and wisdom written on the pages of this wonderful book by Doug Malear – Signs Along the Way.

–Phil McClain, Founding Pastor / Director
Western Michigan Teen Challenge

Without hope people cannot move forward. God at work in the lives of His people makes everyone stop and wonder about the amazing power of grace. The stories describing God at work in the lives of Doug and Sui and the folks at Hope Lighthouse generates hope, the power needed for anyone looking for a good reason to keep pushing forward, yea God.

–Ruston Seaman, Pastor of Peoples Church, Philippi, W. VA
Director of New Vision,[1] Re-energizing Communities

Signs Along the Way is a great thought provoking compilation of the signs of "our" time. Pastor Malear has great insights into the mindset of our culture and compares them to the truth of God's Word. Pastor Doug and Sui Malear are great people and true servants of the Lord. They have a heart for God like very few that I have ever met.

–Apostle Steven A. Bach, Author and President of Encouragement
Ministries International

Signs Along the Way is a delightful, pithy read that challenged me at points and had me laughing out loud at others. You will so enjoy Doug's writing style and will only complain as you finish that there wasn't more to read.

–Ed Gungor, New York Times best-selling Author Pastor of
Sanctuary Church in Tulsa, OK General Overseer, cmiGLOBAL

Signs Along the Way is an interesting read for every believer and especially for new believers. My friend and co-worker in the Faith, Doug Malear, captures the Christian pathway through interesting and often amusing marquees. Every Church in America needs to give this book to new Christ followers as a means of establishing their new walk of faith.

–Rev. Dennis L. Kutzner, Pres., Cert Risk Assessor
Fort Wayne, IN GlobalChurchConnection.com

Have you ever considered the word "rare"? It means very uncommon, scarce. Every once in a while you and I will run across something or someone who fits that description. Doug Malear certainly falls into that category. He is a loyal friend, a passionate man of God, and a gifted writer. He is humorous and observant in Signs Along the Way. His gift of seeing things that others do not, and his ability to express life changing thoughts in an easily read manner will endear this book to your heart and make you desire to share it with many others.

–Robert Rogers, Speaker, writer
Founder of Foundational Ministry Center

This is a book that well reflects the character and devotion of a man who has experienced more of this world than any of us would ever want to and has come out a trophy of God's grace through it all.

–Doug Bytwerk, Sr. Pastor
First Baptist Church of Spring Lake

Don't give up on your loved ones; it is well with my soul. God reached down into Detroit's 'Cass Corridor', plucked a junkie from the streets, and made him a leader of men with a passion to save souls in the inner city.

–Douglas E. Malear (the author's father) He wrote this shortly
before passing into the Lord's eternal arms in April, 2010.
He pursued the author with God's grace for twenty three
years before he wrote this joyous endorsement.

To mom and dad who never gave up on me,
and to my wife Sui, who still inspires me.

CONTENTS

INTRODUCTION

A pastor I know once remarked, "All my sermons come from church marquees." The statement was intended to be humorous, but there is actually a deeper truth going on in that declaration as well. Many of us go to church and enter the building on Sundays to hear a biblical message, but these days you can read a biblical message without ever entering the building. All you have to do is drive by the church. There are thousands of these marquee messages dotting the landscape of our nation. Many of them, though short, pack a powerful punch. They are the proverbs of our times, the news of the day, and a look into our culture. They are glimpses along the way into the psyche of the American condition at the end of the twentieth century and the beginning of the twenty-first century.

For a number of years now, I have been privileged to travel to churches and communities throughout Michigan, Illinois, Indiana, and Ohio. I have traveled to represent our inner-city ministry and to share stories of real people whom the life-saving gospel of Christ has helped and changed. I say "privileged" because I am so grateful to be able to preach to many congregations and raise much-needed funds for our mission at the same time. My background of homelessness, heroin addiction, prison, and finally reconciliation to the Lord has allowed me to proclaim the gospel message in a way that a wide variety of people can relate to. During my travels, I developed an interest in the *signs along the way* (billboards and marquees), so I began to photograph them. It got to be a fun way to pass the time while driving through different towns, villages, and open stretches of highway. I would be on the lookout for new and thought- provoking messages wherever I went. Today, I have these pearls of wisdom captured in hundreds of photographs.

These signs, found on the marquees of churches, gas stations, car washes, and in some unusual places, have short, simple pro- verbial messages to impart to passing motorists. The messages are many and varied. They say everything from, "Jesus is the reason for the season" to "Smoking won't send you to hell, but will make you smell like you've been there." They are not all intended to convey a biblical message. But on further reflection, I've learned that many of them put forth a Bible truth without mentioning God or the Bible. Some are humorous and help to lighten our load as we travel the serious, burdensome highways of this life. Some give us food for thought and help us reflect on the different avenues we have tra- versed, as well as those we have yet to embark upon. Then there are those that point us to something larger than ourselves and remind us of the "big picture"—they point us to God.

I began to write some commentary and add a Bible verse to go with each sign that I photographed. I wrote what I felt the message was conveying to me and perhaps to the world at large. Many of them prompted me to do some deeper research before writing their stories. Some brought personal experiences long forgotten to the surface of my mind and onto the page. I hope they will be helpful to believers and seekers alike along their respective journeys for meaning and truth. I hope also that some of them will cause you to smile as you identify yourself and recognize the humor in these signs that define the human condition.

I like to keep my camera close and ready to shoot these special glimpses into the American wit and spirit. I see them as a kind of barometer of the times we live in and the directions we take as we erect our *signs along the way*. I want to share them with you here, and pray they remind you of the big picture.

Doug Malear

Hope Lighthouse Ministries

Part 1

SIGNS OF SALVATION

But of that day and hour no one knows, not even the angels of heaven, but My Father only.

– Matthew 24:36

ALL EXPENSES PAID

When I was younger, about a million years ago, I received a three-year, all-expenses-paid trip, to Jackson Penitentiary in Jackson, Michigan. This prison was opened in 1839 (before I got there) as the state's first prison (Michigan State Prison). The first permanent structure was constructed there in 1842, but was relocated to a new building in 1926. Soon after, it became the largest walled prison in the world with nearly six thousand inmates.

The original structure actually housed Civil War prisoners, but unlike the Civil War prisoners, I was not incarcerated for a cause I believed in enough to put my life on the line. I was a criminal. The last thing I was willing to do was lay my life down for any cause or anyone. I grew up in the "me" generation, and it most assuredly, was all about me at that time in my life. Sometime later I met someone who laid down His life for me and many others, but before I elaborate, let me go back a little bit.

I was finishing high school back in 1969. In those days everything was anti-establishment, peace, love and marijuana. This was before Christ (BC) in my life, and I was drifting about without much direction. The problem with that lifestyle, like anything else you practice, is that it's progressive. You can predict the general results of a life by the things practiced and established early in that life. Unless something drastic happens, the chance of changing the destiny of that life is slim. In my case, anti-establishment went from a social or civil mind-set to one of breaking the law; peace and love morphed from a worldview to a personal license for premarital sex without accountability; and marijuana progressed from a social pastime to a full-blown heroin addiction with all the darkness and ugly baggage that goes with it. During the years I lived and worked on staff at Teen Challenge we coined this phrase to describe how progressive sin is; Sin will take you farther than you want to go, keep you longer than you want to stay, and charge you more than you are willing to pay.

Looking back, that is exactly the way it happened. In the beginning, it was exciting, adventurous, and felt like I was charting unknown territory. If you had asked me then if I would eventually sell drugs or steal to support an addiction, I would have answered, "Of course not." But day by day, step by deeper step, I was going farther than I ever thought I would. I found myself in situations I would not have even considered being a part of at one time. And it was costing me everything – my dignity, my self-respect, my reputation and my ability to change course. I felt like I was on an all-expenses-paid ship heading for death and destruction, but I could not get off. My strength and resolve were too weak. I needed help, rescuing – I needed a Savior.

Scripture says that no man knows the day or the hour when Jesus will return. It also tells us we can be sure where we will spend eternity. The book of Romans in the Bible informs us in chapter 10 and verse 13; "Whoever calls on the name of the Lord shall be saved". When Jesus told the well-respected Jewish leader and teacher Nicodemus that he must be born again to get into heaven (John 3:3), He was explaining to him what it meant to be saved.

The marquee sign here is advertising an all-expenses-paid trip to paradise (heaven). No one in the history of the world could pay for that trip, no one—that is, but Jesus, the Son of God. He was the only truly righteous person without sin who ever walked the earth. He therefore was eligible to pay the price to open the way to heaven for all of mankind.

> Jesus said to him, "I am the way, the truth, and the life. No one comes to the Father [heaven] except through Me."
> —John 14:6

Most people do not know when death will overtake them in this life, which is why the sign proclaims, "Departure times vary." But even though most do not know when their time on earth will come to an end, I reiterate, everyone can choose where they will spend eternity. God has given us the gift of free choice. The implication in the latter part of the sign, "Departure times vary," is not only do most of us not know when we will depart from this life, but we also need to do a check to see if we are prepared to cross over to the other side. We do not know, for the most part, when our departure time will come about, but we can know that we are ready to meet our maker.

> Living in the light of eternity changes your priorities.
> —Rick Warren

When Jesus was hanging on the cross near death, a thief hanging near Him acknowledged that Jesus was Lord. Jesus told him, "Today you will be with me in paradise." In Jesus' conversation with Nicodemus in the book of John, chapter 3 and verse 15, He informed Nicodemus that whoever believed in Him (Jesus) would not perish but have eternal life. And then in verses 16 and 17, He said, "For God so loved the world that He gave His only begotten Son, that whoever believes in Him should not perish but have everlasting life. For God did not send His Son into the world to condemn the world, but that the world through Him might be saved."

I mentioned earlier that I met someone who laid down His life for me and many others. That someone was Jesus, whom I met sometime after I got out of prison (many years ago), and my life made a 180 degree turn. I have, and everyone who puts their trust in Jesus has, that all- expenses-paid trip to paradise. Because Jesus paid the fare, I am on an exciting journey through life and on my way to heaven. On this journey, I get to live for Jesus and to make Him known to those I journey alongside until my own departure time is announced.

Bible Baptist Church

GOD HAS THE BEST FIRE INSURANCE PLAN

Sunday School 9:45am · Worship 11am & 6pm · Wed. Prayer AWANA 7pm

> Save others by snatching them from the fire; to others show mercy, mixed with fear—hating even the clothing stained by corrupted flesh.
> —Jude 1:23 NIV

GOD'S FIRE INSURANCE

Wow! This is a strong message if you look beyond the surface to what is really being conveyed. I'm sure most of us know God is not some cosmic insurance salesman who is trying to get us to buy His fire insurance because it's better than AAA or Nationwide or some other national insurance company. Obviously, this sign is a somewhat humorous way of saying, "Choose God's plan to avoid hell." But with deeper thought, it has very serious implications. When I think of God having such an insurance plan, I start to imagine Him in an office somewhere with a sign or marquee over the door that asks, "On your way to eternity, would you prefer smoking or nonsmoking, heaven or hell?"

But that's just my warped mind at work. The truth is, God doesn't want anyone going to hell. He made hell for the devil and the fallen angels who followed him, not for men and women. Men and women make their own choices on that matter. God, in His infinite love and wisdom, has given us the gift of free will. This free will puts the choice of how we will live totally under our control. God will never (although He could) force anyone to accept His fire insurance, even though it is not His will for anyone to end up in hell.

[God] is longsuffering toward us, not willing that any should perish but that all should come to repentance.

$$-2 \text{ Peter } 3:9$$

Can anyone really know for sure where they will end up? Does God really have a "fire insurance" plan that gives absolute assurance? How much would something like that cost? Would anyone be able to get it, and is there really some kind of "get out of hell free" card? Yes, yes, yes, yes, and no on the card. The Bible teaches that we can know where we will spend eternity. In Romans 10:9 and 10, we read the promise that backs up God's insurance plan for us: "That if you confess with your mouth the Lord Jesus and believe in your heart that God has raised Him from the dead, you will be saved. For with the heart one believes unto righteousness, and with the mouth confession is made unto salvation." That is God's plan. He sent His only Son, Jesus, to take all of our sins upon Himself and to receive our punishment by dying on the cross, thereby giving us an out. He was the only one who could do it because He was the only one who ever walked the earth completely sinless. He became the perfect sacrifice to save us from an eternal hell.

A common fire insurance policy is provision against losses caused by fire and lightning. The insurer agrees, for a fee, to reimburse the insured in the event of such occurrences. The standard policy limits coverage to the replacement cost of the property destroyed, less a depreciation allowance. Indirect loss, such as that resulting from the interruption of business, is excluded, but it may be covered under a separate contract. Insurance rates are influenced by the quality of fire protection available where the building is located, the type of building construction, the kind of activity conducted within the building, and the degree to which the building is exposed to losses originating outside it.

> Religion is insurance in this world against fire in the next.
> –Anonymous

The beauty of God's insurance plan is that it is really a preventative measure. With other fire insurance policies, you have to pay up front and then face fire and loss before you can collect. The difference with God's plan is far and above better than all the rest. Nothing else comes close. First, you pay nothing up front; you just accept the payment Jesus made at the cross. Second, you never experience fire or loss, but you still collect the benefits of the policy. Third, the quality of your protection is not dependent on what you do, who you are, or what you have. It is top-of-the-line coverage for all who desire it. Finally, there are dividends for those who accept this policy, dividends all along the way and long before the final payoff.

Those dividends come in the form of a renewed life–a life of peace, contentment, and victorious living. The really great thing about this insurance is that your price never changes, your policy never expires, and again, you never face the fire in order to collect. God does have the best fire insurance, and it's affordable and available to anyone and everyone who chooses it.

GOD CAN MAKE ALL THINGS NEW - EVEN YOU

Therefore, if anyone is in Christ, he is a new creation;
old things have passed away; behold,
all things have become new.

–2 Corinthians 5:17

GOD MAKES ALL THINGS NEW

God can and does make all things new. It's kind of His thing, and He's just so good at it. The marquee message ends by saying "even you." That means you and me. According to the verse below the sign, the new life is conditional upon being in Christ. In the New Living Translation of the Bible, 2 Corinthians 5:17 is translated like this: "This means that anyone who belongs to Christ has become a new person. The old life is gone; a new life has begun!"

However you read it, that's good news! I wonder how many people at some time in their lives have wished they could start fresh and do things differently. That is exactly what Christ is offering every one of us, a chance to become brand-new. He is offering each of us a chance to start again, to be kinder, more loving, at peace with ourselves and our surroundings. I just could not believe it was possible. I had always believed that you could not teach an old dog new tricks. I was sure that by the time people became adults, they were set in their ways and could not change. But whereas it certainly seemed nearly impossible for me, it was not impossible with God!

I have heard it said that 85 percent of the people who come to know Christ as their Savior do so by age eighteen. That sounds awfully dismal for many of us who are older. I was quite a bit over eighteen when I came to Christ. I was self-centered and hardheaded toward God as an adult for a long time and never thought I could change even if I wanted to. God seems to specialize in changing old things into brand-new things. All through the Bible, we see Him making new things from old things, things we would not have given a second glance.

> We keep moving forward, opening new doors, and doing new things, because we're curious and curiosity keeps leading us down new paths.
> —Walt Disney

Louis E. Boone[1] said it like this, "Don't fear failure so much that you refuse to try new things. The saddest summary of a life contains three descriptions: could have, might have, and should have." The Bible has a lot to say about new things. Here are just a few of them:

He [God] has put a new song in my mouth

—Psalms 40:3

Behold, I will do a new thing, now it shall spring forth; shall you not know it? I will even make a road in the wilderness and rivers in the desert.

—Isaiah 43:19

You shall be called by a new name, which the mouth of the Lord will name.

—Isaiah 62:2

I will give him a white stone, and on the stone a new name written which no one knows except him who receives it.

— Revelation 2:17

Through the Lord's mercies we are not consumed, because His compassions fail not. They are new every morning; great is Your faithfulness.

— Lamentations 3:22–23

Likewise He also took the cup after supper, saying, "This cup is the new covenant in My blood, which is shed for you."

— Luke 22:20

Neither do people pour new wine into old wineskins. If they do, the skins will burst; the wine will run out and the wineskins will be ruined. No, they pour new wine into new wineskins, and both are preserved.

— Matthew 9:17, NIV

When the Lord saves a man or a woman, He makes them new. He has to make them new in order for His Spirit to live in them. He could not sustain His Spirit in them if they did not become new in the process. No, He needs a new man or new woman in which His Spirit may dwell. What I mean by that is a man or woman who has chosen to ask for His Spirit. He does not force His Spirit on anyone, but the Spirit is always available to all who choose to accept Him. They become brand-new; the old passes away, and they are then ready to live the abundant life of the saved. This is the abundant life that Jesus promised in John 10:10: "The thief does not come except to steal, and to kill, and to destroy. I have come that they may have life, and that they may have it more abundantly." The new thing that God is doing in us prepares us not only for heaven, but also for life here and now. He gives us power to overcome the enemy of our souls and power to live a Christ-centered life.

Then He who sat on the throne said, "Behold, I make all things new."

–Revelation 21:5

Then they said to one another, "We are not doing
right. This day is a day of good news, and we
remain silent. If we wait until morning light, some
punishment will come upon us. Now therefore,
come, let us go and tell the king's household."

—2 Kings 7:9

GREAT NEWS

We don't just have the "good news." We have the "great news."

I was driving down the street one day when I saw a person in a bear outfit advertising insurance in front of a local company. The bear was carrying a sign that read, "GREAT NEWS!" The purpose behind the bear suit and sign was to attract new customers. This type of picture was my bread and butter, so to speak, the kind of opportunity I could not pass up. I stopped to snap a picture, and it turned out that the person in the bear outfit was a young lady whom I knew from a local church. She recognized me right away and then told me who she was. I explained that I wanted the picture to write about the good news, which to us, as followers of Christ, really is the great news.

The word *gospel* in the Bible describes four books that give an account of the life, death, and resurrection of Jesus Christ. The books are Matthew, Mark, Luke, and John, which are referred to as the Gospels in the Bible. The word *gospel* actually means "good news." That good, or great, news is spelled out clearly in the Scriptures;

By this gospel you are saved, if you hold firmly to the word
I preached to you. Otherwise, you have believed in vain. For
what I received I passed on to you as of first importance: that
Christ died for our sins according to the Scriptures, that he
was buried, that he was raised on the third day according to
the Scriptures, and that he appeared to Cephas, and then to
the Twelve. After that, he appeared to more than five hundred
of the brothers and sisters at the same time, most of whom
are still living, though some have fallen asleep.

– 1 Corinthians 15:2–6 NIV

That is the great news. He went through all of that in order to
give us fulfillment on earth and a home in heaven. Even in the Old
Testament of the Bible, we see types of the good news that would
eventually come through Jesus Christ. There is a story in the book of
2 Kings about the good news. In chapter 6, we read that the city of
Samaria in Israel was surrounded and under siege by Ben-Hadad, the
king of Aram (Syria), and his entire army. They had conquered most
of the little towns in the area and were now starving the inhabitants
of Samaria and waiting for them to surrender.

The people in Samaria were Israelites, God's chosen people,
but they had strayed far from God and His commandments. They
seemed to have forgotten the good news that God loved them. The
famine in that city got so bad that people were actually eating their
babies. We don't believe something like that could happen in twen-
ty-first-century America but we have been killing unborn babies by
the millions since it became legal in 1973. I was a teenager during
the flower-power generation of the sixties, and if someone had said
to us that in a few short years our country would make abortion on

demand legal, we would not have believed it. What is incredible to me today is that there are people who have been born, grown up, completed college, started families, and are in our workforce who have never known a time when abortion was not legal in America.

These people in Samaria were the religious people of the day, and the armies attacking were their enemies. Their real problem was on the inside, not the outside. It was a heart problem. If they had been right with God, they would not have shrunk in fear from their enemies.

> If there is no enemy within, the enemy without
> can do you no harm.
> –African proverb

There is a similar story in 2 Kings 19 that took place in Jerusalem, where Hezekiah was king. The Assyrian army under King Sennacherib surrounded Jerusalem. They outnumbered the fighting men in Jerusalem, and as with Samaria, they had already taken the smaller towns nearby. The difference in the two stories is that when they were under siege by the enemy, King Hezekiah went into the house of the Lord and prayed for deliverance. The Bible tells us that an angel of the Lord killed 185,000 enemy troops that night. The next morning all who were left of the Assyrians fled for home.

Now, if we look back at 2 Kings 7:3, we see that there were four men with leprosy at the city gate of Samaria. Leprosy, in the Old Testament of the Bible, is often used metaphorically for sin. These four men were not accepted inside the city by the religious people, and if they went out beyond the gate, the enemy army was there. They were caught between a rock and a hard place. They were caught between the "church crowd," who were religious but not righteous, and the godless enemies of their day, who were trying to take over their community. Why does that have such a familiar ring to it? Just sayin'.

They finally decided to go to the camp of the enemy. They reasoned together, "If we go into the city, we will starve to death with that church crowd. If we stay here, we'll starve and if we go to the enemy, we could be imprisoned or killed." They were so hungry and at the end of themselves that they thought that even if they were killed, they might get fed first. They decided to surrender to the enemy.

I have to wonder how many people in our society, who are labeled misfits, drug addicts, alcoholics, etc., are not accepted by the church of today and decide to surrender to the enemy of their souls. Has the church become an exclusive club in our time? The example that Jesus taught was that we are to love people regardless of their flaws, bad choices, or lifestyles. Jesus did not condone sinful behavior, but He changed lives through His incredible love. As followers of Christ, we are called to model that incredible love and bring good news to a lost world. Through that kind of love, we may gain a platform from which to share the great news and also have credibility when we stand up as a body of believers for our Christian values.

When the four lepers reached the enemy camp to surrender, they found it empty. God had intervened and caused the enemy to flee the camp, leaving most of their possessions behind. The lepers went from tent to tent, gathering food, clothing, gold, and silver. They kept hiding the plunder for themselves and coming back for more. But after a while they stopped and declared to one another in 2 kings 7:9; "We are not doing right. This day is a day of good news, and we remain silent. If we wait until morning light, some punishment will come upon us. Now therefore, come, let us go and tell the king's household."

We who call ourselves Christians have the good news. If we keep it to ourselves until Jesus returns, punishment may come upon us. The question is, are we keeping it to ourselves, or are we sharing it with the world that God loves so much He gave His Son for it?

We have great news. Let's share it!

This year thousands of men will die from stubbornness.

Learn the preventive medical tests you need. ahrq.gov

AHRQ

The fool has said in his heart, "There is no God."

–Psalm 14:1

MEN DIE FROM STUBBORNNESS

Thousands of men die every year without knowing Jesus as Savior. Thousands of men and women around our planet go to the grave every year not having had a born-again experience with the Lord of all life. This is not just people who have never been told about Jesus. I'm talking about those who have heard the gospel but have stubbornly rejected the message of the cross. That was me at one time. It seems like a lifetime ago and unreal. My pride always got in the way. The notion that I made my own destiny, shaped my own world, and that I was in charge was stubbornly and deeply ingrained in me.

> None are so empty as those who are full of themselves.
>   – Benjamin Whichcoat

Oh, yes! It was definitely all about me. I called the shots, made the decisions, went after what I wanted, and did it with gusto. Mac Davis, a country western and pop singer, described it so well in the 1980 hit song he wrote called "Lord, It's Hard to be Humble".

Oh, Lord, it's hard to be humble

When you're perfect in every way

I can't wait to look in the mirror

'Cause I get better lookin' each day

To know me is to love me

I must be a hell of a man

Oh, Lord, it's hard to be humble

But I'm doin' the best that I can[1]

Those are just part of the lyrics, but you can see the theme. It was a tongue-in-cheek humorous song, but at the same time, it made a real statement about our stubbornness toward the Lord and our propensity to rely on self.

It takes a humble attitude to surrender your life to Jesus. I was at a place in my life where I had basically lost everything that was important to me. It was through my own foolishness, but it served to bring me to a place of openness to the Lord. There are still far too many people dying in our world without knowing Jesus, but I thank God I am no longer one of them. And it's a great joy to me, telling others about His saving grace.

According to wholesomewords.org the actual number of people who die each year globally is about 55.3 million. The same source informs us that there are more than twice as many births as deaths each year in this world of over 7 billion people. There are over a thousand deaths every ten minutes around the world, or 151,600 each day. Even if only 10 percent die without knowing Jesus that would be an incredible 5.5 million people each year. I am far from being a math major, but if that many people died without Christ in the United

States each year, in two to three generations that rate would claim the entire population of the nation.

In Proverbs 5:21–23, the New Living Translation Bible says, "For the LORD sees clearly what a man does, examining every path he takes. An evil man is held captive by his own sins; they are ropes that catch and hold him. He will die for lack of self-control; he will be lost because of his great foolishness." The last line of this scripture could say "He will be lost because of his great stubbornness".

In many poor countries around the world people are more open to the gospel of Christ because they have so little to get in their way. Some of these folks are living in primitive conditions without electricity, good water, or an adequate food supply. They do not see a bright future for themselves or the chance for a better life on this earth because their concentration is just to survive another day. In the United States, most of us don't fight for our survival each day. We grow up surrounded by things we take for granted, things we just assume will be there for us every day, things like clean and plentiful drinking water, stores filled with food of every variety and open just about any hour of the day. A pastor friend of mine tells the story of the time friends of his from Russia came to visit him. He took them to a Wal-Mart store one day. When they entered the store and saw the rows upon rows of every kind of food in such abundant quantities, they began to weep.

At the touch of a button, we have electricity, air conditioning, heat, washing machines, dryers, coffeemakers, micro-wave ovens, etc. These are just the tip of the iceberg, but you get the drift. We have so many labor and time saving devices (distractions) that keep us busy maintaining them, that we can miss what is really important. We are so blessed compared to the majority of the world. But it's also our abundance of material blessings that distracts us from needing the Lord while also building up our stubbornness toward the gospel.

We are also encouraged to chase the American dream in order to acquire all the bells and whistles; the home, two cars, a boat and all the toys that go with it. A big part of the American dream is relying on self, doing it and having it your way, pulling yourself up by your boot-straps, and making it work according to your truth. That is just the opposite of how we come to Christ. Unfortunately, we have somehow equated the American dream with Christianity, as though they are the same. Nothing could be further from the truth. Christianity, or being a Christ-follower, has nothing to do with our strength, intelligence, abilities, or stuff we accumulate. It has everything to do with humbling ourselves, dropping our stubbornness, and surrendering our lives to the Savior, Jesus Christ.

Oh Lord, it's hard to be humble

And if it seems evil to you to serve the Lord, choose for yourselves this day whom you will serve, whether the gods which your fathers served that were on the other side of the River, or the gods of the Amorites, in whose land you dwell. But as for me and my house, we will serve the Lord.

−Joshua 24:15

YOU HAVE A CHOICE

You're gonna serve Somebody

– Bob Dylan

This sign on a medical-supply company informs us that we have a choice as to where we purchase this kind of product. Then, of course, it encourages us to choose their company. The scripture in Joshua also puts forth a choice to us, an eternal choice. God gives every human the gift of free choice. He does not force us to obey, serve, or worship Him. He makes it totally a matter of choice, our choice.

Whereas Joshua tells us to choose whom we will serve, Dylan makes it emphatic when he says we will serve somebody. We truly will choose, whether by action or inaction. We are faced with choices all of our lives. From the cradle to the grave, we make choices from what to eat for breakfast, whether to go to college, to picking a mate. The type and quality of the life we live will depend largely on the daily and long-term choices we make.

The first choice I make every day is whether to get out of bed, or go back to sleep. There are times when I feel like the man who prayed, "Lord, it's been a good day so far. I haven't said a cross word to anyone, argued for my way, coveted the possessions of others, or cut in front of anyone in traffic. But Lord, I'm about to get out of bed........." So yes, we make multiplied conscious and unconscious choices throughout our day.

> We like to think that life is happening to us rather than life is happening as a result of the choices we make.
>
> – Devlyn Steele

I resonate strongly with Steele's quote above. Life is happening as a result of the choices we make. It puts the responsibility on us. Are you beginning to understand how these choices multiply throughout the day with very little effort? They just keep coming and we make many of these routine choices almost automatically. We really don't have to think much when making many of them. I think that's why I sometimes do things like, pass the street I usually turn onto because I expected my automatic pilot to make the choice. Oh sure, we can't choose what the weather will be, or which team is going to win the championship (of course there are those who say they can). Suffice it to say, there are many choices beyond our control, but also many that we have been given the opportunity to decide upon.

Some statistics tell us we make upwards of 3,000 to 3,500 minor, medium, and major choices every day. These choices strung together day after day, month after month and year after year add up to shape our lives, define our journeys, and ultimately make us who we are. Our journey is ongoing, which means we can change who we are by making different choices.

We also choose whether to overcome the negative things that come our way or surrender to them. Stephanie Marston, author and motivational speaker writes, "You have many choices. You can choose forgiveness over revenge, joy over despair. You can choose action over apathy."[1] So along with the choices we make about what to do or not do, what our attitude will be in whatever situation, or what our response will be, we also make choices about how to think. "For as he thinks in his heart, so is he" (Proverbs 23:7). We can choose to love, to forgive, and to go the extra mile, by changing our thinking, pursuing righteousness, believing, and living out the scriptures.

I can do all things through Christ who strengthens me.

—Philippians 4:13

In Proverbs 9, we see a great example of being confronted with a choice. This particular choice is between wisdom and foolishness, with the end result being life or death. In verses 1 through 6, wisdom calls out to all who are simple (foolish or ignorant) to follow her and live. Conversely, in verses 13 through 18, foolishness calls out to all who are simple to follow her, but in the end it leads to death.

Read both passages for yourself here:

Wisdom has built her house, she has hewn out her seven pillars; she has slaughtered her meat, she has mixed her wine, she has also furnished her table. She has sent out her maidens, she cries out from the highest places of the city, "Whoever is simple, let him turn in here!" As for him who lacks understanding, she says to him, "Come, eat of my bread and drink of the wine I have mixed. Forsake foolishness and live, and go in the way of understanding."

—Proverbs 9:1–6

A foolish woman is clamorous; she is simple, and knows nothing. For she sits at the door of her house, on a seat by the highest places of the city, to call to those who pass by, who go straight on their way: "Whoever is simple, let him turn in here"; and as for him who lacks understanding, she says to him, "Stolen water is sweet, and bread eaten in secret is pleasant." But he does not know that the dead are there, that her guests are in the depths of hell.

—Proverbs 9:13–18

The choice here is life or death, spiritual life or death. Every one of us will ultimately make the decision to either come to God through Jesus Christ's sacrifice on the cross, or we will reject Him. The choice is ours.

Part 2

SIGNS OF TRUST

ALWAYS OPEN

CLOSED

A man who has friends must himself be friendly, but there is a friend who sticks closer than a brother.
—Proverbs 18:24

ALWAYS OPEN

Doctors, counselors, and most other professionals have what we call "office hours," which are usually in the 9:00 a.m. to 5:00 p.m. time frame. They are not "always open," as this sign suggests. They have a designated, understood time to open and a time to close. The word *always* never precedes the word *open*. You cannot go to them after their regular, designated closing time, and everyone understands that.

The message on the sign was humorous (at least to me) because of the conflicting messages. The same sign that advertised they were "always open" also proclaimed they were "closed." The important thing to me here is that these messages illustrate the difference between going to God and going to man. First of all, going to man can get you more confused than you were before you went. But God is truly always open and ready to meet you right where you're at.

Man will let you down at some point. People will turn their backs on you, disappoint you, break their promises, and close on you. That is the nature of finite man. Words like *always* and *never* are extreme claims. The person saying them is in effect claiming to know the future by proclaiming this will "always be" or "never be."

We have learned, once again, in the United States recently that the economy is fickle. You cannot count on it, and you certainly cannot put your trust in it. A store doing great today could go under next month. The owner of the sign *Always Open* clearly put it up originally to be a permanent message, fully expecting to be open always, 24/7. Something obviously happened to change that. It could have been any number of things or a combination of things, but whatever or whoever the owner put his trust in let him down.

In the Bible, Deuteronomy 31:8 states, "And the LORD, He is the One who goes before you. He will be with you. He will not leave you nor forsake you; do not fear nor be dismayed." And again in Joshua 1:5, the Lord says, "As I was with Moses, so I will be with you. I will not leave you nor forsake you." Those are promises from God that you can rely on, promises you can build your life around with confidence.

The owner thought that because business was so good, it would stay that way and he would never close or have a lack of customers. He trusted that the good times would continue indefinitely, but one day the economy tanked. Something changed drastically in his life, or some unforeseen thing happened, and he had to close his doors. It may not have been anything he did wrong, but he put his trust in something that was temporal, something he relied on, believed in.

We know that running a business can be a bit unpredictable at times. You can put everything you have into it, have tremendous faith in it, and still see it go south on you. My point is, no matter how much you believe in temporal things and put your trust in them, they are still just temporal. But the Bible says that there is a friend who will stick with you closer than a brother and, as mentioned earlier, will never leave or forsake you.

> Never be afraid to trust an unknown future to a known God.
> – Corrie ten Boom

The question we have to ask ourselves periodically is, who or what am I putting my trust in? I say "periodically" because things around us in our temporal world change all the time. They are constantly evolving for good and for bad. Products may change, methodology may differ, strategies do improve as man learns more about his world, and people change as they grow and mature. What doesn't change is God. James 1:17 says in the New Living Translation, "Whatever is good and comes down to us from God our Father, who created all the lights in the heavens. He never changes or casts a shifting shadow."

I think it is a good idea to revisit our core beliefs on a regular basis to stay on center. We, as humans, have a tendency to be swayed in different directions by any number of enticements and temptations. It reminds me of the story in Greek mythology of the Sirens. The Sirens were dangerous and beautiful creatures portrayed as femme fatales. They would lure nearby ships and sailors with their enchanting music and their voices that were eerie, but mesmerizing. Finally, the ships would be shipwrecked on the rocky coast of their island.

Many things in our modern world, like the mythical Sirens, promise so much but deliver so little. They promise one thing, but once we are fully engaged, we find out it is something totally different. Sin in our lives does that also. The word *sin* comes from an old archer's term that means to miss the mark. Sin, then, is missing God's best, to get off track.

God's plan for us is to get back up and move forward despite the circumstances. God wants to encourage us just as He encouraged the Israelites in Jeremiah 29:11: "For I know the thoughts that I think toward you, says the Lord, thoughts of peace and not of evil, to give you a future and a hope."

This verse was written to encourage the Jewish people who were taken captive to Babylon for seventy years. Jeremiah was telling them to trust the Lord because He had a good plan for them. We too can put our trust in the Lord today regardless of our external circumstances. The world offers everything, but in the end, it cannot deliver. But there is a friend, the Scriptures say, who sticks closer than a brother.

God never closes.

EVENINGS AT 7
IN THE PARISH HALL

MON	ALCOHOLICS ANONYMOUS
TUE	ABUSED SPOUSES
WED	EATING DISORDERS
THU	SAY NO TO DRUGS
FRI	TEEN SUICIDE WATCH
SAT	SOUP KITCHEN

SUNDAY SERMON
9 A.M.
"AMERICA'S JOYOUS
FUTURE"

Weeping may endure for a night, but joy
comes in the morning.
—Psalms 30:5b

AMERICA'S JOYOUS FUTURE

When I first saw this sign in front of a church the messages for Monday through Saturday seemed like a huge contradiction to the Sunday sermon. Monday through Saturday advertised a list of help services for many of the woes that are plaguing our society today. It somewhat defines where we're at and even who we are as a country. But then, at the end of that list, Sunday proclaimed that America has a joyous future. That's the contradiction.

Reading that list of social ills was anything but joyous. It was a list detailing the results of a permissive "do your own thing" society that seems to have lost its moral compass. Our society is drowning in a sea of overindulgence, a desire for instant gratification, and a self-induced blindness to consequences. In other words, we are reaping what we have sown. Let's take a closer look at the daily help groups that were offered on the sign.

Mondays and Thursdays: Drug and Alcohol Abuse

Drug and alcohol abuse have shipwrecked many souls. It has become epidemic in America. Rehabilitation programs dot the landscape like never before and have become a very lucrative business for some. Does this sound like a joyous future? I beg to differ.

In 2012, an estimated 23.9 million Americans ages twelve or older—or 9.2 percent of the population—had used illicit drugs in the past month.[1]

There were just over 2.8 million new users of illicit drugs in 2012 (about 7,898 new users per day). Fifty-two percent of those were under eighteen.[1]

In 2012, 30.4 percent of males twelve and older and 16 percent of women reported binge drinking (five or more drinks on the same occasion) in the past month.[1]

Tuesdays: Spousal Abuse

Spousal abuse is on the rise in this country. The joyful celebration of a man and woman devoting themselves to each other in the presence of God, family, and close friends too often becomes unbalanced and combative as they live together. It is anything but joyous.

One in four women will experience domestic violence during their lifetimes.[2]

Women experience more than four million physical assaults and rapes at the hands of their partners, and men are victims of nearly three million physical assaults.[2]

Every year, one in three women who are victims of a homicide is murdered by her current or former partner.[2]

Wednesdays: Eating Disorders

Teens in America are dealing not only with obesity, but other eating disorders as well.

About 525,000 US teenagers are struggling with eating disorders:[3]

Anorexia 55,000

Bulimia 170,000

Binge-eating disorder 300,000

Fridays: Teen (and Youth) Suicide

There are more pressures on teenagers than ever before, and many of them are having trouble coping with the demands that are placed on them.

Suicide is the 2nd leading cause of death for ages 10-24.[4]

There has been an alarming 128% increase in suicides for ages 10-14 since 1980[4]

Each day there is an average of over 5,400 suicide attempts in grades 7-12.[4]

More teenagers and young adults die from suicide than from cancer, heart disease, AIDS, birth defects, stroke, pneumonia, influenza, and chronic lung disease combined.[4]

Saturdays: Soup Kitchen

Many people and families need help with food these days. Our own food pantry, located in a high-poverty area, serves about five hundred families each month. Feeding America, a national food bank, says that about one in six Americans struggles with hunger. Things seem to be getting worse rather than better. It's not just in America, but around the world.

You will hear of wars and rumors of wars, but see to it that you are not alarmed. Such things must happen, but the end is still to come. Nation will rise against nation, and kingdom against kingdom. There will be famines and earthquakes in various places. All these are the beginning of birth pains.

—Matthew 24:6–8

Do these things mean Christians should just be concerned for themselves and wait for Jesus to return? Does this mean that there is no hope and we can do nothing to change the course of the world? I would say, "No!" There is too much Scripture to the contrary. Christians are to be salt and light, soul-winners. There can be a joyous future for everyone, not just in America. It is not contingent on external circumstances, but on internal peace that comes from knowing Jesus as Savior. Philippians 4:6–7 teaches, "Be anxious for nothing, but in everything by prayer and supplication, with thanksgiving, let your requests be made known to God; and the peace of God, which surpasses all understanding, will guard your hearts and minds through Christ Jesus."

Jesus told us to love one another so that our joy would be full. All believers may look forward to a joyous eternal future with Jesus in heaven, as well as an abundant life right here on planet earth. In John 10:10, Jesus said, "The thief does not come except to steal, and to kill, and to destroy. I have come that they may have life, and that they may have it more abundantly." The first part of the verse reminds us that we live in a fallen world with evil all around us. Satan's plan is to steal, kill, and destroy. He will use alcohol, drugs, eating disorders, spousal abuse, suicide, etc. (all the things on this church marquee and more) to shipwreck our lives and separate us from God. But they who truly have the Son (Jesus) are free. They are free to live an abundant, joyous life in the physical realm while looking forward to a joyous future that is to come.

And again, the psalmist declares, *"Weeping may endure for a night, but joy comes in the morning."*

LIFE IS NOT ABOUT HOW TO SURVIVE THE STORM BUT HOW TO DANCE IN THE RAIN

> Dear brothers and sisters, when troubles come your way, consider it an opportunity for great joy. For you know that when your faith is tested, your endurance has a chance to grow.
> —James 1:2–3 NLT

DANCING IN THE RAIN

Have you ever danced in the rain, or kicked at and splashed the water puddles along your path while laughing out loud in the process? You might well say, "Yeah, when I was a kid." There is something very freeing about dancing in the rain as an adult. The fact that you are dancing in an environment that has sent everyone else running for cover is empowering. You are throwing off restrictions that would normally dictate how you are to react in such a situation.

We learn, as we grow into adulthood, that we are to come in out of the rain because of the negative aspects of not coming in: we'll get wet or cold, mess up our hair and our clothes, and maybe even get sick, thereby creating unnecessary trouble for ourselves. So we learn that trouble and tribulation are to be avoided at all costs. I think part of what James is saying in this verse is that we should count trouble as joyful for what God and the trouble can teach us, if we embrace it.

I am not advocating seeking out problems, but Jesus said, "In this world you will have trouble. But take heart! I have overcome the world" (John 16:33). We will have trouble. It's not a possibility; it's an absolute certainty. In this fallen and broken world, we will encounter problems. James teaches us that by facing our troubles with the right attitude and information, we can count it an opportunity for joy. In other words, we can dance in the rain.

Children, quite often, will innocently dance in the rain and count it all joy, unconcerned with the potential negative aspects or danger associated with the coming storm. And they are oblivious to what others may think. Those things are not obstacles or hindrances to them because it's about enjoying the adventure. Actually, the rain and the mud puddles are more of an unexpected and welcome surprise to their day, a refreshing opportunity to grab hold of. I believe that is part of the attitude or thought James is conveying here when he tells us to consider problems as an opportunity for great joy.

It's also about an attitude of expectancy, expecting great things to come from great challenges. It's not about hunkering down in the storm and doggedly, by the sheer force of your will, surviving it. It's about genuinely looking at the experience with new eyes, from a totally fresh perspective with an attitude that asks, "What am I going to learn from this? What is God working together for good in this situation?"

In Revelation 3:19, God said, "As many as I love, I rebuke and chasten: be zealous therefore, and repent" (KJV). In the Berkeley translation, the latter half of that verse reads like this: "So burn with zeal and change your attitude." Your attitude will determine how you view, handle, and finally resolve the diverse situations that come with life. Attitude also plays a huge part in your health and the health of your relationships.

> A bad attitude is like a flat tire. If you don't change it, you'll never go anywhere. —Anonymous

The interesting thing about the sign I photographed for this writing is that my car broke down after I took the shot. I was on my way to a three-day conference in Fort Wayne, Indiana, and was traveling south through Kalamazoo, Michigan, when I decided to get off the highway for coffee. I saw the sign in front of an insurance company, so I drove into their parking lot, turned off my car, and got out my camera. The trouble started after I got the shot.

I got back into the car, turned the key, and it would not start. I called my road service and waited for about an hour for a tow truck to show up and pull my car to a repair place. While I was waiting for the truck, I was thinking, *It's late in the afternoon. I probably can't get my car fixed until tomorrow, and I'm going to miss the first evening of the conference.* I knew that I was also far from home and had nowhere to stay for the night. I was definitely having a bit of trouble, or in other words, I was experiencing one of life's storms. And all the while I was sitting next to this great marquee sign that declared, "Life is not about how to survive the storm, but how to dance in the rain."

The whole situation was priceless and showed me once again how the Bible is my source for living life and knowing the Savior of my soul. The situation had James 1:2 all over it: "Dear brothers and sisters, when troubles come your way, consider it an opportunity for great joy" (NLT). James was not telling us to enjoy the trouble for itself, but for what it can produce in us as we follow Christ.

My car and I made it to the repair garage in downtown Kalamazoo just before closing. I was informed that they would look at it first thing in the morning. I thought it might be as simple as replacing the alternator (turns out I'm not much of a mechanic). I found a hotel just blocks away, got a good night's sleep, and came back in the morning. It wasn't the alternator. It was more major (and more costly) than I had initially anticipated, and it was going to take four or five hours to fix.

It was a beautiful, clear, and warm end-of-summer day, so I walked through the downtown area, taking in the sights. I bought a hot dog from a street vendor, found a bench, and sat there thanking God for His creation. Then I spent the rest of the day in the Kalamazoo library, reading and doing some work on my lap-top computer. I got a late-afternoon call from the garage to inform me that my car was done and the cost was eight hundred dollars. I had already missed that day's workshops and talks at the conference, but I made it there for the evening service and all of the workshops and speakers the next day.

But that's not the end of the story. I had called the general secretary of our fellowship while I was in Kalamazoo to let him know my situation. I told him I would be there as soon as my car was finished and ready to carry me to the conference. During my time at the conference, at different times various ministerial brothers who had heard about my car trouble began to put money in my hand to help defray the cost of my car-repair bill. I told no one how much the repair bill had come to. The interesting thing is that what they gave me added up to $817.

Don't ya just love it, dancing in the rain?

WWW.CALVARYBIBLEMUSKEGON.ORG

Calvary Bible Church

SUNDAY SCHOOL
9:30 A.M.

WORSHIP SERVICE
10:30 A.M.

DUSTY BIBLES LEAD TO DIRTY LIVES

All Scripture is given by inspiration of God, and is profitable for doctrine, for reproof, for correction, for instruction in righteousness, that the man of God may be complete, thoroughly equipped for every good work.
—2 Timothy 3:16–17

DUSTY BIBLES

A great majority of American households have at least one Bible somewhere in their homes. It may, in some cases, be sitting on a shelf, gathering dust from disuse. It may be buried away in some long forgotten drawer or the dark recesses of a closet. Some people actually prominently display a large, ornate family Bible on a coffee table or counter for all to see, but rarely or never open its pages to read.

A couple of years ago, I read somewhere that Christian households in America have, on the average, somewhere between four and seven Bibles. But while America has an overabundance of Bibles (and almost everything else), there are countries in our world yearning for Bibles. In China, for example, there are 200 million Christian believers without Bibles, according to Bob Drew, who is with Bibles for China. International Christian Concern projects that China is on track to be the largest Christian nation in the world just a couple of decades from now.

Today in America, about 75 percent of adults identify themselves as Christian. In comparison, the next largest religions in America are Islam and Judaism. Combined they represent only about 1 to

2 percent of the population of the United States.[1] Part of being a Christian is regular Bible reading. It is nourishment for the soul. Without it, we become spiritually depleted, our lives are weakened, and we are more prone to evil temptations. According to Gordon-Conwell Theological Seminary, approximately 83 million Bibles are distributed globally each year and there are approximately six million books about Christianity in print today.

People in Asia and countries where Bibles are scarce or outlawed seem to have a greater hunger for the Bible than most of us who have unlimited access to the Bible. Our needs are too easily met through other means. We have such abundance that we tend to take it for granted. Many Americans go to large churches that have developed professional-looking, huge stage performances that rival most theaters. They have musicians with state-of-the-art sound, video productions, light shows, smoke machines, comfortable theater seats, etc., all to cater to the people attending.

In David Platt's best-selling book *Radical*, he tells of being taken under cover to a secret underground Asian house church to teach the Bible. There were about sixty people crowded into a room, not big enough by our standards, waiting for him. There was one bare lightbulb for illumination and no music, projector screens, or video. Many sat on the floor or on little stools. All they had was the Word of God and they were hungry for its truths. Platt says he taught for many hours every day for about ten days, and they just could not get enough. *All they had was the Bible.*

It ain't those parts of the Bible that I can't understand that bother me; it is the parts that I do understand.

—Mark Twain

75

I wonder if our churches would fill up to capacity and more if all we offered was to open, teach, discuss, and share the Bible. That's where the rubber would meet the road. No stage shows, no performances, no cutting-edge videos, no famous people up front and no lattes. There is nothing intrinsically evil about any of these things, unless they become as, or more, important than God and His Word. In America, Christianity has come under fire because of the hypocrisy of those who call themselves Christian but don't live it. The more that Christian people rely on their own understanding rather than getting instruction from the Bible, the more their Christianity will be watered down.

Trust in the Lord with all your heart, and lean not on your own understanding; in all your ways acknowledge Him, and He shall direct your paths.

—Proverbs 3:5–6

Whenever a large part of any society begins to move away from biblical teaching, morals start to slip. And because things are always progressive, that society will become progressively more sinful. The dog you feed will be the dog who grows big and strong. Over the years, by allowing our Bibles to gather dust, our society has spiraled downward as we moved away from biblical standards and treated sin as no big deal.

> Sin will always take you farther than you want to go, keep you longer than you want to stay, and cost you more than you want to pay.
> – Teen Challenge Idiom

In America, nearly 40 million public school students were participating in daily public prayers until we outlawed it in 1962 with the *Engle vs. Vitale* court ruling. We made the aborting of unborn babies legal in 1973 with the *Rowe vs. Wade* court ruling. Then people started petitioning to have plaques that display the Ten Commandments forcibly taken out of courtrooms, school-rooms, and public spaces. Many things that we have held important in this country as foundational standards to live by are being attacked as Bibles gather dust in our homes.

Within the covers of the Bible are the answers for all the problems men face.

— Ronald Reagan

In 1 Samuel chapter 8, a similar thing took place with the Israelites. The Lord had freed them from slavery and led them into the Promised Land flowing with milk and honey. Their society was called a theocracy because it was God led. Then the people decided they did not want to be led by God; they wanted a man to be king over them. They could identify with a man of flesh and blood who would put desires of the flesh above the things of God. From that time on, their existence was up and down like a roller coaster. They, like us, wanted God out of the way so they could satisfy their sin nature by doing things their way.

And as the marquee states, *"Dusty Bibles lead to dirty lives."*

BE PREPARED...
IT WASN'T RAINING
WHEN NOAH BUILT THE ARK!

Heaven and earth will pass away, but My words will by no means pass away. But of that day and hour no one knows, not even the angels of heaven, but My Father only.
—Matthew 24:35–36

NOAH WAS PREPARED

To be prepared in life is a good thing. The more prepared we are for the projects, choices, and everyday circumstances of life, the more ready we will be when the storms and troubles of life come our way. And be assured, they will come, because they are part of life on planet earth.

Speaking of being prepared, I was actually a Boy Scout for a brief period as a teenager. We learned a lot about character, camping, and getting along with others. Their motto was "Be prepared." Looking back, I can see now how appropriate that motto was. Everything we did was preparing us to live our lives in a responsible and upright way. It was great preparation for adulthood.

> We will always remember. We will always be proud. We will always be prepared, so we will always be free.
>
> —Ronald Reagan

God told Noah to build an ark when he was five hundred–plus years old. A careful reading of Genesis 5:32 through Genesis 7:6 reveals that it took Noah the better part of a hundred years to build the ark. He went into the ark with his family the year he turned six hundred.

Along with his family, Noah loaded the ark with two of every kind of animal. All those animals living on the ark with less than ideal bathroom facilities must have made it a pungent experience. This may be how the doubtful story of Mrs. Noah's complaint got started. It seems that after many weeks at sea, things were getting pretty ripe on the ark. Mrs. Noah came to Noah one day and complained, "It stinketh in here!" to which Noah replied, "Yes, but it's the best thing afloat."

The task of building the ark was huge, and Noah did not have a lot of help. He had three sons who were probably quite young when he started the project. They grew up around the building process and most likely became a great help to their father. The good thing was that Noah had great preparation. God gave him the exact measurements to make it, how to build it, what to put in it, and the type of material to use. God was the designer, and He gave Noah lots of time to do the job.

When God first came to Noah with the plan, it must have sounded very strange. Noah probably asked, "What's an ark?" God might have explained that the ark was to be the first cruise ship the world had ever known, or He might have just told him it was a big boat. Then He might have told Noah it was going to rain nonstop day and night for forty days, at which time Noah would have asked, "What's rain?" You see, it had not rained on the earth before this, so Noah would not know what rain was. They got their water and moisture through dew, underground streams, and fountains that would come to the surface and water the earth. In comedian Bill Cosby's account of the story, whenever Noah would get frustrated and stubborn about building the ark, God would ask him, "Noah, how long can you tread water?"

Then, of course, there were Noah's neighbors, who watched him building the ark over the years. He would have told them he was preparing for a great flood, a great judgment upon the earth. They obviously did not believe him because none of them helped or entered the ark to save their lives when the rains came. They may have thought he was crazy, but Noah's building of the ark and his reason for doing so were a witness to his neighbors of his strong belief in God.

But even if you should suffer for what is right, you are blessed. Do not fear their threats; do not be frightened. But in your hearts revere Christ as Lord. Always be prepared to give an answer to everyone who asks you to give the reason for the hope that you have. But do this with gentleness and respect.

—1 Peter 3:14–15

> A man who lives fully is prepared to die at any time.
> —Mark Twain

Though the Bible tells us that no one knows the day or the hour when Jesus will come back, we are encouraged to stay prepared, to be ready just as Noah was. Scripture tells us to live our lives ready for Jesus' return because He will come like a thief in the night. House burglars do not call and make an appointment to rob your house; they come totally unexpected. I remember a great song called "I Wish We'd All Been Ready" by the late Larry Norman. Part of the lyrics went like this:

Life was filled with guns and war

And everyone got trampled on the floor

I wish we'd all been ready

Children died, the days grew cold

A piece of bread could buy a bag of gold

I wish we'd all been ready

There's no time to change your mind

The Son has come and you've been left behind

A man and wife asleep in bed

She hears a noise and turns her head, he's gone

I wish we'd all been ready

Two men walking up a hill

One disappears and one's left standing still

I wish we'd all been ready

There's no time to change your mind

The Son has come and you've been left behind[1]

If you can accept this, the ark in Noah's time was a type of the Christian church today. Just as the ark was Noah's family's sanctuary and a safe haven from the storms, flood, and violence of a sinful world, the church of today is our ark. It is a place of nurture, growth, and safety. It was not raining when Noah started building the ark, but because God told him to be prepared for rain and a flood, he obeyed, getting himself and his family prepared. They were saved because they believed God.

Are you prepared if Jesus comes back today? I hope we'll all be ready!

Part 3

SIGNS OF WITNESS

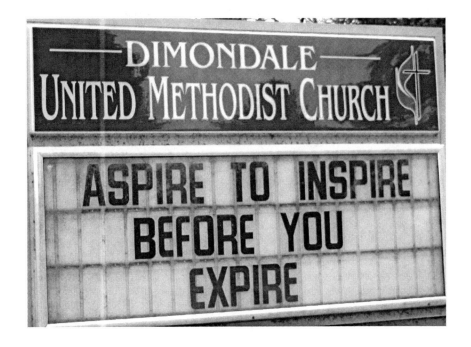

I must work the works of Him who sent Me while it is day; the night is coming when no one can work.
—John 9:4

ASPIRE, INSPIRE, EXPIRE

The words on this marquee encourage us to do something with our lives while we are able, to use our time to inspire those around us. In the gospel of John, Jesus said something similar in chapter 9 and verse 4. His disciples had just asked Him if the blind man they encountered was blind as a result of his sin or his parents' sin. Jesus explained that the man's blindness was not a result of anyone's sin, but a part of God's grand design, that through his healing God would be revealed and glorified. Jesus informed them that as long as He was in the world, He would be the light of the world, implying that without Him our world would be a very dark place. Then He did what He does so well. He proceeded to heal the blind man.

Alleged "impossibilities" are opportunities for our capacities to be stretched.

—Charles R. Swindoll

I'm sure you've heard the expression "Make hay while it is day." I believe part of the message to us here is that we need to see and recognize opportunities before they have a chance to slip away. Many things in our world are cyclical, like times and seasons, in that they repeat themselves or come around again. Sometimes they give us second or third chances to do what we missed the first time around. But there are no guarantees that we will get another shot.

It's easy to procrastinate when you're young and think you are going to live forever, or at least another fifty to sixty years. You tend to think you have plenty of time to do the right thing tomorrow or next week or next year. We know at a factual level that tomorrow is not promised, but at the same time, we think, *My life won't be cut short. I've got lots of time.* Because of that kind of thinking, some folks never accomplish what God has planned for them on this earth. The truth is, all we really have is this moment. Yesterday is gone, and tomorrow's not promised.

Behold, now is the accepted time; now is the day of salvation.
—2 Corinthians 6:2

If we continue to put things off, there will come a day when such opportunities will be gone forever. There is wisdom in the old adage "Don't put off until tomorrow what you can do today." You don't know what unexpected things may pop up to claim your time tomorrow. Don't put things off. They have a tendency to pile up on you. And yes, I'm speaking from experience. Proverbs 3:28 puts it like this: "Do not say to your neighbor, 'Go, and come back, and tomorrow I will give it,' when you have it with you."

Whitney Houston was internationally known for her phenomenal voice and was often referred to as one of the best female pop singers of all time. She died totally unexpectedly on February 11, 2012, at age forty-eight. Elvis Presley was an American singer, musician, and actor. He was one of the most significant cultural icons of the twentieth century. He is often referred to as the "king of rock and roll." He died unexpectedly on August 16, 1977, at age forty-two.

Both Whitney and Elvis proclaimed that Jesus was Lord, although their lifestyles did not always bear that out. They had fame and fortune, could buy whatever they wanted, and go wherever they desired. In the eyes of the world, they had it all. One thing is certain. The day before their deaths, no one, including them, knew they would be dead in twenty-four hours. They had no idea that their window of opportunity to be a blessing, to point others to Jesus, to enjoy family and friends, and to live their lives was about to close abruptly. They may have had plans to change the dangerous parts of their lifestyles but felt they had plenty of time.

> Whereas you do not know what will happen tomorrow.
> For what is your life? It is even a vapor that appears
> for a little time and then vanishes away.
> —James 4:14

James is telling us that life is short on this earth and that compared to living in eternity with the Lord, this life is like a vapor that appears for a hot second and dissipates just as quickly. So with that in mind, we read again the words of Jesus in John 9:4 and realize when He says to us, "The night is coming when no one can work," that our window of opportunity is indeed short and limited during our time on earth. There is surely a day coming for each one of us when night comes and death overtakes us.

The hope that I have, is to not look back and regret missed opportunities, or at least to see that the missed opportunities were outnumbered by the ones I embraced in order to be a blessing in the lives of others. I want to work while it is day, to model and proclaim salvation in Christ Jesus, and to inspire others before I expire.

> Be very careful, then, how you live—not as unwise but as wise, making the most of every opportunity, because the days are evil.
>
> —Ephesians 5:15–16

ILLITERATE?
WRITE FOR FREE HELP.
ILLITERACY FOUNDATION
806 MAIN STREET

Do you see a man wise in his own eyes? There is more hope for a fool than for him.
—Proverbs 26:12

ILLITERACY

This billboard is an oxymoron. It seems ludicrous and somewhat foolish to advertise "in writing" when the audience you are trying to reach is illiterate. It is asking those who cannot read or write to first of all read the sign and then write for help—duh! An *oxymoron* is defined as a figure of speech that produces an incongruous, seemingly self-contradictory effect, as in "cruel kindness," "to make haste slowly," "accidentally on purpose," "authentic reproduction," and so on.

Merriam-Webster's online dictionary defines the word *illiterate* in the following way: "having little or no education; especially: unable to read or write." The apostle Paul said in 1 Corinthians 13:1, "Though I speak with the tongues of men and of angels, but have not love, I have become sounding brass or a clanging cymbal." In other words, if we as Christians do not communicate with love, we may as well be illiterate.

If you are reading what I am writing here, it tells me two or maybe three things:

1. You can read.
2. You understand the English language.
3. You are probably Christian, especially if you continue reading.

Let's look at this third point. Because I am writing in a Christian publication to Christians, it's reasonable to assume my readers are Christian. But beyond that, there may be something deeper and less obvious at first glance. What I mean is, my language will be sprinkled with words and terms understood in large part by Christians, but not necessarily by non-Christians. I use terms from the Bible that are familiar in Christian circles. I believe that part of being a Christian is inviting people to know Jesus (or to see Jesus in us) in everything I do in an easily understood way. And that should include my writing. So as I write this, and knowing the subject I am presenting, I am more aware of making my writing understood by those outside the Christian camp.

In this case, as I said, I am writing to a mostly Christian audience. But I am wondering about our conversations with those in the marketplace, the workplace, the school place, and the public square who may not be Christians. How can we be salt and light to the lost if they cannot even understand us? If we simply blurt out to them, "You're lost," they may answer, "No, I'm not. I know exactly where I am." If we come across as judgmental in proclaiming that they need to "get saved," they may counter with the question, "Get saved from what?"

I think Paul's words in 1 Corinthians give us our first clue; that is, no matter our language or how many languages we speak, if it is not coming from a place of genuine care and love, we might as well be making a clanging, unintelligible noise. When we are operating on a foundation of love and grace, we will choose to use words that develop bridges rather than gulfs between us.

You can never understand one language until you understand at least two.

—Geoffrey Willans

Proverbs 18:21 states, "Death and life are in the power of the tongue." We need to be sensitive in our speech to the unchurched. They don't speak "church." We won't always get it right, but people usually respond in positive ways as we speak to them right where they're at in genuine honesty and caring. Jesus said, "But I say to you that for every idle word men may speak, they will give account of it in the day of judgment. For by your words you will be justified, and by your words you will be condemned" (Matthew 12:36–37).

We can get so wrapped up in church, church activities, and church friends that we forget there are millions of people throughout the world who do not speak our language but are in desperate need of our Savior. Paul showed us a great illustration when addressing unbelievers in Acts 17:16–34. In verses 16–17, the Scriptures say, "While Paul was waiting for them in Athens, he was greatly distressed to see that the city was full of idols. So he reasoned in the synagogue with both Jews and God-fearing Greeks, as well as in the marketplace day by day with those who happened to be there."

Paul did not shy away from talking with these unbelievers, because he genuinely cared for their souls. He not only reasoned with people in the synagogue, or church, but he also conversed with nonbelievers in the marketplace on a regular basis. When you read the whole section, it shows how Paul spoke the truth in love and how he quoted from their own poets rather than talking over their heads with some theological mumbo jumbo. It shows how he looked for common ground from which he could begin an open and meaningful dialogue.

Paul did not win them all to his way of thinking, but he got them talking and thinking about the things he said. Some of them even became believers. None of them listened to Paul because they thought he was superior to them or because they feared him. They listened because Paul was willing to meet them on their own turf and to hear what they had to say. They listened because Paul did not treat them as illiterate pagans, but as human beings who were loved by God as much as he was.

The rapport the early church had with many of the unchurched is pointed out in chapter 2 of the book of Acts. In verses 46–47, we read: "So continuing daily with one accord in the temple, and breaking bread from house to house, they ate their food with gladness and simplicity of heart, praising God and *having favor with all the people*. And the Lord added to the church those who were being saved" (emphasis added).

People could see, whether they came to faith or not, that these church people had something very special. They were a joy to be around and easy to communicate with. Does the general public feel that way about the Christian church today? As Christians in the world today, we need to look at the unchurched as those who are illiterate and need our love and help to find the truth.

REAL WISDOM IS HAVING SOME-THING TO SAY AND KEEPING IT TO YOURSELF

Marne United Methodist Church

He who has knowledge spares his words, and a man of understanding is of a calm spirit. Even a fool is counted wise when he holds his peace; when he shuts his lips, he is considered perceptive.

—Proverbs 17:27–28

KEEP IT TO YOURSELF

We are living at a time in history, the twenty-first century, when English is the most widely spoken and written language on earth. It is the official language in 83 countries/regions and spoken in 105 other countries. Curiously, the English language does not have official status in Australia, the United Kingdom, and the United States.

English was first spoken in Britain by Germanic tribes in the fifth century AD, also known as the Old English (Anglo-Saxon) period. Old English initially was a diverse group of dialects, reflecting the varied origins of the Anglo-Saxon kingdoms of Britain. Invasions by Normans and others in the eighth and ninth centuries helped develop the language at the start of what is called the Middle English period (1150–1500). European languages, including German, Dutch, Latin and ancient Greek influenced the English vocabulary during the Renaissance (1400–1700). We are now in the Modern English period, which started in the sixteenth century.

The number of words in English (according to Johnny Ling, 2001) has grown from fifty thousand to sixty thousand words in Old English to about a million today. With all the words available to us today, most of us have something to say in most situations, but the wise among us know when to keep it to ourselves. There have been times in my life (believe it or not) that I have shared openly what I thought was wisdom at the moment and later wished I'd kept that little nugget to myself. Those were usually instances when I didn't take much, if any, time to think about what I was saying. But words and how we use them are very important.

> Understand this, my dear brothers and sisters: You must all be quick to listen, slow to speak, and slow to get angry.
> —James 1:19

It truly is wisdom to keep our mouth shut at times. The benefit, according to our featured verses (Proverbs 17:27–28), is that we may seem wise to others. The added benefit is that with our mouth firmly shut, it's harder to fill it with our foot or say something we'll regret. Someone has said, "It's better to keep your mouth shut and possibly be thought a fool than to open it and remove all doubt."

In this electronic age of communication with e-mail, texts, tweets, etc., we need to be especially careful not to make declarations and statements without thinking about what we are saying. Sometimes our mind (or at least my mind) has the tendency to shoot from the hip by allowing things to come out of our mouth without first hanging out in our brain for a moment. It's like a knee-jerk reaction to things that are said to us at times, as we answer quickly and automatically. We are seeing more and more teens with cell phones sending text messages and pictures that they regret later. But once they send it, they can never take it back or prevent the whole world from potentially seeing it.

When we are talking face-to-face with someone and we say something wrong or derogatory, we wish that we could just say, "Disregard that last statement as though I never said it." But the truth is, it's out there, was heard, and cannot be taken back. When you document something through texting or sending pictures, it becomes potentially amplified. Not only does the immediate hearer get the message, but also it is recorded for any number of people at any time to receive what you have put out there. These electronic devices and social media are a large part of how our young people communicate today, and for their own peace, protection, and safety, they will have to learn to apply certain user etiquette.

We should hear and purpose to practice James's advice in chapter 1 and verse 19 to be quick to listen, slow to speak, and slow to become angry. "Silence is golden," sang the sixties and seventies' British rock group the Tremeloes, which is part of the point James is making. Sometimes silence is exactly what is called for. The verse mentioned earlier (Proverbs 17:28), in the Message, a paraphrase of the Bible in contemporary language, puts it quite graphically: "Even dunces who keep quiet are thought to be wise; as long as they keep their mouths shut, they're smart." On a related point, studies in the past claimed that women talk more than men, but a contemporary study has concluded that as of 2013, both men and women speak an average of 16,000 words per day.[1]

There are two major things that help me with my written responses to communications I receive, particularly if they seem derogatory or conflicting. One is to be slow to answer so I can pray and/or meditate on what a godly response would look like. Second, I run it by my wife. She gets to hear my first, unthinking, unedited, quick response. Then she begins to lovingly point out some things I should be giving more thought to, saying differently, or not saying at all. She likes to remind me of who I am in Christ and encourages me to craft my responses in a loving Christlike manner. Many times that means keeping it to myself.

Marne United Methodist Church

YOU ONLY LIVE ONCE - BUT IF YOU DO IT RIGHT, THAT'S ENOUGH

The thief does not come except to steal, and to kill, and to destroy. I have come that they may have life, and that they may have it more abundantly.

—John 10:10

IS THERE LIFE BEFORE DEATH?

s there life before death? Anyone who believes in eternal life or the hereafter will tell you there is life after death. The apostle Paul said that to be absent from the body is to be present with the Lord, and the Bible teaches that after this earthly life, we will live forever in eternity. But what about before we leave this life? Is there life before death, or are we just born, follow some predestined routine, and then die? Are we just puppets, playing out a predetermined destiny that we have no real control over? Are we just waiting, with our heads in the sand, to get through this life, not really living it? I want something a bit more meaningful in this life, and I believe the Lord expects more than that from us. I want to truly live a life that matters, a more abundant life.

> You only live once, but if you do it right, once is enough.
> — Mae West

It seems that many people are just floating through this life looking lifelike, but not really engaged or living the life of abundance Jesus offers. I'm not sure that was the point Mae West was making, but I do love her quote above. Jesus said He came to give, not only life, but life more abundantly. The original Greek for the word *abundantly* in John 10:10 is *per-is-sos'*, and it means "exceeding some number or measure or rank or need; over and above, more than is necessary, something further, more superior, extraordinary, surpassing, uncommon, more remarkable, more excellent." He uses this full and lengthy description to impress upon us that He wants us to live life fully invested and fully alive in this world. He wants us to live life out loud, without fear, and fully embracing all that He has for us here as well as in the life to come. We may know that there is life after death, but Jesus desires us to experience life more abundantly before physical death.

Life is what happens while you are busy making other plans.

—John Lennon

I don't totally know all that Lennon meant in his quote, and I like good surprises, but I want to be intentional about my life. There are plenty of times in life when our plans change because of life's circumstances, but I want to have a mission and a purpose. In the movie *Braveheart*, actor Mel Gibson plays the part of the fourteenth-century historical Scottish hero William Wallace. A well-publicized line that Wallace uses in the movie is "All men die; few men ever really live." William Wallace lived during a time of civil unrest in Scotland. After John Balliol, who held the throne of Scotland for a brief time, relinquished his kingship, Edward I of England had control of Scotland and ruled over the Scots with a heavy hand. Wallace rallied his countrymen and inspired them to fight for their freedom, to lay down their lives for it. He himself was executed in 1305, but he lived life to the fullest by

107

giving himself fully to standing up for his beliefs. I wonder how many of us are actually living our lives to the fullest, to the point that we are willing to die reaching for that abundant life promised by our Lord.

> All men die; few men ever really live.
> —William Wallace in *Braveheart*

It's been said that every morning when the sun comes up on the African plain, a gazelle wakes up and knows that to survive another day it must run faster than the fastest lion. Also, every morning when the sun comes up on that same plain, a lion wakes up and knows that to survive this day it must run faster than the slowest gazelle. It does not matter whether you are a gazelle or a lion; when the sun comes up, you'd better be running. The point is that whatever our place or position in life, we need to be fully engaged participants to survive, run the race, and flourish. So when the Son comes up in your life, you can run the race of the high calling of God in Christ Jesus.

The apostle Paul says to us in Hebrews 12, "Let us run with endurance the race God has set before us." Sitting on the sidelines watching life go by while waiting for the promise of heaven is not God's plan for us. Shortly after throwing off the chains of bondage in Egypt, the Israelites wandered in the desert for forty years on their way to the Promised Land. The problem was that it could have been a trip of less than two weeks. Rather than living their newfound freedom to the fullest, they were plagued by fear, indecision, superstition, disobedience, and a failure to take responsibility for their own destiny. They let the devil travel along with them.

Jesus tells us in John 10:10, in the first part of that scripture, the thief (Satan) has come to steal, kill, and destroy. He comes to convince us that we cannot live a victorious, abundant life in Christ. He does this by stealing our inheritance, killing our dreams, and destroying our spirits. We live in a fallen and broken world full of temptation, sin, tragedy and man's inhumanity to man. We as Christians should be living victorious, exciting, and challenging lives, holding back the enemy with one hand and building the kingdom of God (soul by soul) with the other. Believers have been given a number of mandates in the Bible to live full and exciting lives.

We're told in Jude 23 to snatch others out of the fire.

In Matthew 10, we're instructed to be wise as serpents and harmless as doves.

In Luke 9, we're exhorted to take power and authority over all demons and to cure diseases.

In Acts 1:8, we are encouraged to receive Holy Ghost power to be global witnesses for Jesus.

In Romans 8, we are said to be more than conquerors.

In Philippians 3, we are commanded to rejoice in the Lord always.

In Colossians 3, we are admonished to set our minds on things above.

In Titus 2, we are told to say no to ungodliness.

In James 1, we are encouraged to count it all joy in trials and tribulations.

In 2 Peter 1, we are instructed to be partakers of His divine nature.

In 1 John 4, we are taught to love one another.

And in Revelation 2, we are exhorted to be overcomers.

Despite these biblical directives, Satan, the father of lies, continually tears down and deceives us into believing we don't measure up, that we are not good enough, and that God cannot use us. He tries to squash our dreams and convince us that we have no life. He wants to prevent us from realizing and fulfilling our God-given destinies. The good news that we have to grasp is that Satan is a liar and God has promised us an abundant, fulfilled life. The Bible says the promises of God (to you) are yes and amen (so be it).

Is there life before death? It depends on whether you're living or just existing.

Marne United Methodist Church

**LOOSE TALK
IS NOT THE
SAME AS
FREE SPEECH**

Let no corrupt word proceed out of your mouth, but what is good for necessary edification, that it may impart grace to the hearers.
—Ephesians 4:29

LOOSE TALK—FREE SPEECH

There was a popular saying during World War II, *Loose lips might sink ships*. It was an American English idiom meaning "Beware of unguarded talk." We usually hear or see it today in its shortened version shown in this graphic, but the slogan was actually *Loose Lips Might Sink Ships*. The slogan was in use by 1942 and was one of several similar slogans which all came under the campaign's basic message–'*Careless Talk Costs Lives*'. [1]

The phrase was created by the War Advertising Council and used on posters by the United States Office of War Information. The posters were used in the general campaign of American propaganda during World War II. They were part of a campaign to advise servicemen and other citizens to avoid careless talk concerning secure information that might be of use to the enemy. As someone has said, "Be sure to taste your words before you spit them out."

—Millions volunteered or were drafted for military duty during World War II. The majority of these citizen-soldiers had no idea how to conduct themselves to prevent inadvertent disclosure of important information to the enemy. To remedy this, the government established rules of conduct. The following is excerpted from a document given to each soldier as he entered the battle area.[2]

WRITING HOME

THINK! Where does the enemy get his information — information that can put you, and has put your comrades, adrift on an open sea: information that has lost battles and can lose more, unless you personally, vigilantly, perform your duty in SAFEGUARDING MILITARY INFORMATION?

THERE ARE TEN PROHIBITED SUBJECTS
[we have listed 5 of them here for brevity]

1. Don't write military information of Army units — their location, strength,, materiel, or equipment.
2. Don't write of military installations.
3. Don't write of transportation facilities.
4. Don't write of convoys, their routes, ports (including ports of embarkation and disembarkation), time en route, naval protection, or war incidents occurring en route.
5. Don't disclose movements of ships, naval or merchant, troops, or aircraft.

TALK

SILENCE MEANS SECURITY — If violation of protective measures is serious within written communications it is disastrous in conversations. Protect your conversation as you do your letters, and be even more careful. A harmful letter can be nullified by censorship; loose talk is direct delivery to the enemy.

If you come home during war your lips must remain sealed and your written hand must be guided by self-imposed censorship. This takes guts. Have you got them or do you want your buddies and your country to pay the price for your showing off. You've faced the battle front; its little enough to ask you to face this 'home front.'[2]

The British equivalent used variations on the phrase "Keep mum." The gist of the American slogan was that one should avoid speaking of ship movements, as this talk (if directed at or overheard by covert enemy agents) might allow the enemy to intercept and destroy American or Allied ships. There were many similar such slogans, but "Loose lips sink ships" remained in the American idiom for the remainder of the century and into the next, usually as an admonition to avoid careless talk in general.

The corrupt talk mentioned in Ephesians 4:29 is not warning of information leaking to our enemies. It's warning us not to tear down one another and thereby conform to the desire of the enemy of our souls. However, the scripture does not just warn us not to tear down, but encourages us to lift up one another by our speech. James likens our tongue to a ship's rudder; it's a very small member but controls the direction of the entire ship. It has great power. "Death and life are in the power of the tongue, and those who love it will eat its fruit" (Proverbs 18:21).

> It's easier to build up a child
> than it is to repair an adult.
> Choose your words carefully.
> —Anonymous

The apostle Paul encourages us in Philippians to "fulfill my joy by being like-minded, having the same love, being of one accord, of one mind. Let nothing be done through selfish ambition or conceit, but in lowliness of mind let each esteem others better than himself. Let each of you look out not only for his own interests, but also for the interests of others" (Philippians 2:2–4). We are assured that doing this will impart grace to those who hear our talk. You may wonder what is meant by *grace*. Merriam-Webster's online dictionary defines grace this way:

> 1. a: unmerited divine assistance given humans for their regeneration or sanctification.

If we read farther in Ephesians, we come to 4:31–32: "Let all bitterness, wrath, anger, clamor, and evil speaking be put away from you, with all malice. And be kind to one another, tenderhearted, forgiving one another, even as God in Christ forgave you."

Our loose lips of today, then, are the lips that spit out words of hurt and condemnation, words that are used to tear down the hearers rather than build them up. The power we have in the tongue can be used for good or for evil. It can be used as a sword that cuts and destroys or as an instrument of peace and encouragement.

Yes, we are assured of the right of free speech in America, but we as Christians answer to a higher order. The story of Jonathan and David is a good example. Jonathan was King Saul's son and in line for the throne, but if you know the story David actually became king with Jonathan's blessing. In 1 Samuel 18:4, Scripture says, "And Jonathan took off the robe that was on him and gave it to David, with his armor, even to his sword and his bow and his belt."

Jonathan and David became close friends, and Jonathan trusted David so much that he gave him these things that were dear to him. He gave David his robe, perhaps for warmth, but in a deeper sense, it was a sign of Jonathan's royal covering and protection. He also gave him his defensive and offensive weapons, including his sword. Just like the tongue, the sword is a sharp instrument. When Jonathan gave it to David, he was saying in effect, "You can use that sword to slice and dice me, or you can use it to defend me and lift me up." That is exactly the choice we have with our tongues: we can slice and dice folks, or we can defend and lift them up. The ball is in our court; we can choose.

Loose talk can be used to defame, to abuse, to tear down, and to utterly destroy. Free speech is different. In 2 Corinthians 3:17, the Word of God says, "Where the Spirit of the Lord is, there is liberty." There is liberty, or freedom, where the Spirit of the Lord is allowed to flow. Our freedom comes from the Lord if we are Christians. So our free speech must be used in the way that is prescribed by God in His Word: to lift up and bless the hearer while tempered with love.

Now that is free speech!

Part 4

SIGNS OF GOD-CENTEREDNESS

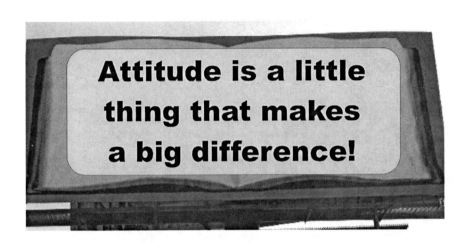

Attitude is a little thing that makes a big difference!

Burn with zeal and change your attitude.
—Revelation 3:19 (TBV)

ATTITUDE IS A LITTLE THING

Webster's New World Dictionary, third college edition, defines *attitude* as follows:

1. The position or posture assumed by the body in connection with an action, feeling, mood, etc.: to kneel in an *attitude* of prayer.
2. A manner of acting, feeling, or thinking that shows one's disposition, opinion, etc.

In the WordNet online dictionary, one definition is as follows: a complex mental state involving beliefs, feelings, values, and dispositions to act a certain way; "His attitude is, work is fun."

Sir Winston Churchill, Britain's fiery prime minister during World War II, is credited as the author of the statement on this marquee. He not only said it, but his life seemed to bear it out. I've heard it said, "Our attitude determines our altitude," or "Attitude is everything." Your attitude at any given time in any circumstance will always affect and even determine results and outcomes.

Attitude is important according to the Bible, but it is also something that can be changed if we desire. Changing one's attitude speaks of changing direction, to make a conscious decision to think and act differently toward something or someone. Revelation 3:19, in the New King James states, "Be zealous therefore, and repent." The New International Version says, "Be earnest, and repent."

The word, *repent* means to change direction and go the opposite way. I like the Berkeley Version of the Bible in this case, because it really gets to the core of what Jesus is saying: "Burn with zeal and change your attitude." Taking this portion of Scripture in context, we see that Jesus was talking to the church of Laodicea. They had a prideful attitude, which was causing them to miss God. They were zealous for the things of the world but lukewarm toward God.

> So, because you are lukewarm, neither hot nor cold, I am about to spit you out of my mouth.
>
> —Revelation 3:16

The city of Laodicea was known during Roman times for its extensive banking establishments, a medical school that had invented a famous eye salve, and a textile industry famous for its rare black wool. This pride of wealth, fame, and material things was not limited to secular society but had spilled over into the church. Rather than influencing their community toward Christ, the church became influenced by the things of the world. We see and experience that same struggle today; the church at large, rather than influencing culture, many times tries to emulate it.

The Laodicean church's attitude openly expressed that they were rich and in need of nothing. Jesus answered their declaration in the following verses: "You say, 'I am rich; I have acquired wealth and do not need a thing.' But you do not realize that you are wretched, pitiful, poor, blind and naked. I counsel you to buy from me gold refined in the fire, so you can become rich; and white clothes to wear, so you can cover your shameful nakedness; and salve to put on your eyes, so you can see" (Revelation 3:17–18, NIV).

Jesus was very thorough in the way that He answered them. He addressed each area that they believed they were excelling in. Their attitude was not one of gratitude to God, but an attitude of "look what we (man) have accomplished." So Jesus told them they were actually wretched and pitiful. Where they boasted of their riches resulting from the extensive banking trade in Laodicea, they were actually poor; where they bragged of their famous, miraculous eye salve and school, they were actually blind; and where they thought they had risen to the top in fashion wear, predicated on a rare black wool produced in their area, they were actually naked.

Jesus is also speaking here to us, the church of today. He knows that we have developed great, intricate programs and structures in our own strength but have left Him out. He knows that we have been building our own kingdoms at the expense of lost souls who need direction to His kingdom. He knows the church, in many cases, has begun to emulate the world, rather than turning the world upside down. He knows that we (the church) need an attitude adjustment now and then in order to get back on track. To quote a famous frog, "It ain't easy being green." Well, it's not always easy being the pure church. We have to work at it, and it starts with an attitude that is open to God, humble, teachable, and willing to take a stand for Christ.

We cannot change our past. We cannot change the fact that people act in a certain way. We cannot change the inevitable.

The only thing we can do is play on the one string we have, and that is our attitude.

—Charles R. Swindoll

Attitude may seem like a little item and not very important in the grand scheme of things, but your attitude can cause you to have a good or bad day, week, year, or life. The attitude you take into the workplace, school place, marketplace, etc. can determine the path you find yourself on and the results realized in every endeavor. If you nurture an attitude of gratitude in your own life and repent; that is, change your attitude from self-centered to God-centered, you will be blessed.

Again, taking these scriptures in context, in the very next verse (Revelation 3:20), we see Jesus standing at the door of the Laodicean church, wanting to be invited in. This verse is often used to show unbelievers that Jesus is standing at the door of their heart knocking, waiting for admittance so He can save their soul.

There is also a well-known painting of that scene that I have seen in numerous places through the years. It is a fascinating piece of modern art painted in 1853–54 by William Holock Hunt called *The Light of the World*. It shows the figure of Jesus preparing to knock on an overgrown and seemingly long-unopened door. In the painting, there is no doorknob on the outside, clearly indicating the person inside needs to respond by opening the door. It is a picture of a patient Christ, indicating a willingness to come into a person's heart and life if the person will open the door of his heart to the Lord.

In these scriptures, He is actually knocking at the door of the Laodicean church and by extension the church of today. The Laodicean church had, without realizing it, left the Lord out of the church. And, of course, it is a great reminder to the church at large today, especially the American church, which, I believe, is in need of an attitude adjustment in order to become the true church of Jesus Christ. Sometimes I feel like we have lost that attitude of gratitude and have traded it for an attitude of self-pride that proclaims to the world, "We have it all together. We can do it all; we have need of nothing." The decision to open the door is in the hands of the church. I pray we will respond to His knocking.

Jesus said in Revelation. 3:20, "Here I am! I stand at the door and knock. If anyone hears my voice and opens the door, I will come in and eat with him, and he with me" (NIV).

For God is pleased with you when you do what you know is right and patiently endure unfair treatment. Of course, you get no credit for being patient if you are beaten for doing wrong. But if you suffer for doing good and endure it patiently, God is pleased with you.

—1 Peter 2:19–20, NLT

CREDIT TO YOUR MAKER?

"How is your credit report?" We see and hear that a lot in our society today. So many things are based on our credit, our track record in financial dealings. Have we paid the debts we took on and promised to pay? Have we consistently made our payments in full and on time according to the payment plan we set up? When most of us go to buy a house, a car, or some other large-cost item, we need to secure financing and set up a payment plan. The very wealthy or the really great savers may be able to pay the full price up front, but again, most of us cannot. So to get financing and set up a payment plan, our credit history is looked at to determine if we have the ability to pay and that we have successfully bought things on credit in the past.

Some definitions for the word *credit* from dictionary.com are as follows:

As a noun:

1. Commendation or honor given for some action, quality, etc.: "Give credit where it is due."
2. A source of pride or honor.
3. Trustworthiness; credibility: a witness of credit.

4. Confidence in a purchaser's ability and intention to pay, displayed by entrusting the buyer with goods or services without immediate payment.

As a verb (used with object):

1. To believe; put confidence in; trust; have faith in.
2. To bring honor, esteem, etc.; to reflect well upon.

There is much more in the dictionary, but you get the idea. When we think of credit, it is usually to do with something financial, but being a credit to our maker is something much different. After reading the question "Are you a credit to your maker?" I personally had to take a deep, hard look at my life and lifestyle. I tried to be very honest with myself. My wife and I run a ministry that deals with the poor, the addicted, and the least in our community. It is our life's work, yet we still have to examine ourselves regularly to gauge whether we are doing it for the right reasons. Are we doing it for accolades for ourselves, or for the Lord and our love for Him?

Jesus said in Matthew 25:35–40:

"For I was hungry and you gave Me food; I was thirsty and you gave Me drink; I was a stranger and you took Me in; I was naked and you clothed Me; I was sick and you visited Me; I was in prison and you came to Me." Then the righteous will answer Him, saying, "Lord, when did we see You hungry and feed You, or thirsty and give You drink? When did we see You a stranger and take You in, or naked and clothe You? Or when did we see You sick, or in prison, and come to You?" And the King will answer and say to them, "Assuredly, I say to you, inasmuch as you did it to one of the least of these My brethren, you did it to Me."

When we help those in need because of our sincere love for Jesus and our desire to emulate Him, we are a credit to our maker. The Bible says it like this in Matthew 6:19–20: "Do not lay up for yourselves treasures on earth, where moth and rust destroy and where thieves break in and steal; but lay up for yourselves treasures in heaven, where neither moth nor rust destroys and where thieves do not break in and steal." Salvation comes through faith in Christ alone. You cannot make heaven your home by doing good things or stacking up credits on earth. We do good works because of our faith in Christ, not to earn our way to heaven.

> Aim at heaven and you will get earth thrown in:
> aim at earth and you will get neither.
> —C. S. Lewis

Being a credit to our maker really has to do with being like Him, modeling His teachings, walking as He walked, and sharing whatever we have with others as He did. When we do those things, we are not only storing up treasure in heaven for ourselves, but we are also bringing credit to our maker. By becoming more like Jesus to the world, we bring credibility and credit to our maker in the world's eyes. They begin to see that it's not all about us and that our lives are truly full and complete as we bring that credit to our maker. It is our witness of Him, walked out in our own lives, that ultimately makes us *a credit to our maker*.

CLEAR CREEK
CONGREGATIONAL CHRISTIAN CHURCH

Pastor Tom Sells
765-584-4387

FAMOUS LAST
WORDS
I DID IT
MY WAY

There's a way of life that looks harmless enough;
look again—it leads straight to hell. Sure, those
people appear to be having a good time, but all that
laughter will end in heartbreak.
—Proverbs 14:12–3 (MSG)

FAMOUS LAST WORDS

One of the most played songs at funerals is "My Way" by Frank Sinatra. Every year it is either number one or in the top three. "I did it my way" are the famous last words of many people who rely only on their own ability. They are in complete control of their destinies and have certainly never surrendered their lives to the lordship of Jesus Christ.

It takes courage to drop our selfishness and pride in order to acknowledge we need help from something bigger than ourselves. Many folks feel they have pulled themselves up by their own bootstraps and lived in a way that was right for them. They could never admit their need of a Savior. In the book of Judges, the Israelites turned their backs on the Lord and wanted to be in control. They wanted no authority or accountability. They wanted to do whatever they desired without boundaries: "In those days there was no king in Israel; everyone did what was right in his own eyes" (Judges 21:25).

The well-known song titled "My Way" was recorded and released by Frank Sinatra in March of 1969. The words of the song were written by Paul Anka and set to music based on the French song *"Comme d'habitude."* Anka bought the rights to the song and rewrote the lyrics with Frank Sinatra in mind. The lyrics tell the story of a man who, having grown old reflects on his life as death approaches. He's comfortable with his mortality and takes responsibility for how he dealt with all the challenges of life while maintaining a respectable degree of integrity.

Frank Sinatra was a Hollywood star and famous singer from the 1950's through the 1980's. But he was more than that. He had a reputation as a tough guy who got what he wanted when he wanted it and from whomever he had to go through to get it. Anka thought it would be the perfect song for Sinatra in the latter part of his singing career. The attitude of pride in doing it alone with no help from God or man was the vein in which he wrote it. The song is about a self-made man who lived life according to his own terms. Here are some of the lyrics:

And now the end is near
And so I face the final curtain
My friend, I'll say it clear
I'll state my case of which I'm certain
I've lived a life that's full
I've traveled each and every highway
And more, much more than this I did it my way.

Regrets, I've had a few
But then again too few to mention
I did what I had to do
And saw it through without exemption
I planned each charted course
Each careful step along the byway
And more, much more than this I did it my way.

Yes, there were times I'm sure you knew
When I bit off more than I could chew
But through it all when there was doubt
I ate it up and spit it out, I faced it all
And I stood tall and did it my way.[1]

This is a description of the macho male image that many of us baby-boomer males grew up with. It's that John Wayne persona that many males were taught to emulate. I believe we inherited it from the Greatest Generation. That model makes it difficult to relinquish any control or humble ourselves by asking for help. It's the stereotypical picture of a man who will not stop and ask for directions, even when lost. This is one of the most requested songs at funerals by men who did not choose to walk with the Lord. Putting our trust in God does not come easy for many of us. Another part of the song makes that clear.

For what is a man, what has he got?
If not himself then he has naught
To say the things he truly feels
And not the words of one who kneels.
The record shows I took the blows
And did it my way.

"Not the words of one who kneels." To kneel to anyone or anything is to be subservient; it's humbling and not very macho. But when we come to God, it must be with humility, acknowledging His lordship.

I am the way, the truth, and the life. No one comes to the
Father except through Me.

—John 14:6

There are many Bible examples of people who did it their way
rather than God's and suffered the consequences. Samson, in the Old
Testament book of Judges, is one of many. He continually abused
the gifts God gave him. He used them for his own gain rather than
for the good of others, which was God's plan. He was eventually
imprisoned and blinded by his enemies until he finally humbled himself and asked God to strengthen him one more time. In his death, he
came back to God, but perhaps missed the full life God had planned
for him.

Someday we will all bend our knee to Jesus: you, me, Frank,
everyone. We get to make the decision whether to do it now and
make heaven our eternal home, or be forced to do it at the judgment
seat of Christ and spend eternity in hell separated from God.

That at the name of Jesus every knee should bow, of those in
heaven, and of those on earth, and of those under the earth.

—Philippians 2:10

I believe that as Christians, we should examine ourselves regularly to be sure the direction we are traveling lines up with God's
way. When our way becomes like God's way, we can then sing with
confidence, "I did it my way."

CROSSROADS CHURCH
UNITED BRETHREN IN CHRIST

FORBIDDEN FRUITS
CREATE MANY JAMS
COME AND WORSHIP
SUNDAY II AM

LAnd the woman said to the serpent, "We may eat the fruit of the trees of the garden; but of the fruit of the tree which is in the midst of the garden, God has said, 'You shall not eat it, nor shall you touch it, lest you die.'"
—Genesis 3:2–3

FORBIDDEN FRUIT

We have all seen and experienced trouble, heartache, and difficulties in our lives as a direct result of doing something we knew we shouldn't be doing. We can include being somewhere we knew we shouldn't be or even hanging out with some folks we knew better than to associate with. The author of the marquee sign here nails it succinctly and with great imagery: "Forbidden fruits create many jams."

The hundreds of millions (make that billions) of jams that people throughout time have found themselves dealing with began way back in the Garden of Eden. It all started with Eve's decision to pick and eat the fruit from the tree that God declared forbidden. Genesis 3:6 says, "So when the woman saw that the tree was good for food, that it was pleasant to the eyes, and a tree desirable to make one wise, she took of its fruit and ate."

Lest we place all the blame on Eve, remember, Adam was with her, and according to the second part of that same verse, "she also gave to her husband with her, and he ate. So, she picked the fruit, ate it and offered some to Adam, which he accepted and ate." We must also remember that in Genesis 2:16–17, before Eve came on the scene, God had told the man this fruit was forbidden: "And the LORD God commanded the man, saying, 'Of every tree of the garden you may freely eat; but of the tree of the knowledge of good and evil you shall not eat, for in the day that you eat of it you shall surely die.' "

Adam and Eve must have had all kinds of different fruit trees to choose from. We don't know how many trees there were, but they were referred to by God as "every" tree. God uses the same word when He tells us He formed "every" beast and "every" bird in Genesis 2:19: "Out of the ground the LORD God formed every beast of the field and every bird of the air, and brought them to Adam to see what he would call them." When we look at the number of beasts and birds there are in the world, we begin to get the big picture.

There was a multitude of trees with good, desirable fruit to choose from every day. God was a God of blessing and abundance, so there could have been hundreds or thousands of different fruit trees to eat from. The Garden of Eden was the perfect paradise before the fall of man. I don't think the types of fruit trees were limited to the types we would find today in the general geographical area most scholars place Eden in. My point is, they had more choices than they would probably ever use, yet they felt to partake of that which was forbidden. Not much has changed in the world between then and now, as far as going after forbidden fruit. And yes, forbidden fruit or things that are not good for us, create many jams, problems, and disconnects in our lives.

I have heard many people say (after making bad choices and facing consequences) things like, "I just knew I shouldn't have gone there," or "Something told me not to do that." But we are like children. No matter how many great fruit trees there are to pick from, we will gravitate to the one that is forbidden to us. There is plenty of fruit that is not forbidden to us, but we usually have to work at it.

> You've got to go out on a limb sometimes
> Because that's where the fruit is.
> —Will Rogers

The jam created by Adam and Eve, when they ate the forbidden fruit, was world changing. Their action spun the world into a place of darkness and sin. The idyllic garden community was no more. And that is the world that you and I were born into and live our lives in—a fallen world.

Man has tried for centuries to devise ways to get back to the garden and back to God, but our best efforts have fallen short each time. The rock group *America* wrote a song about the 1969 Woodstock concert in upstate New York and included lyrics about getting back to the garden:

> Well I came upon a child of God,
> He was walking along the road
> And I asked him tell me where are you going,
>
> This he told me:
> (He) said, I'm going down to Yasgur's farm,
> Going to join in a rock and roll band.
> Got to get back to the land,
>
> And set my soul free.
> We are stardust, we are golden, we are billion year old carbon,
> And we got to get ourselves back to the garden.[1]

The fact is, we don't have within us the power to save ourselves. We can never do enough good works to receive God's grace or go back to the garden and start over. God, however, has not abandoned us. He has a plan. A plan to reconcile us back to Himself. He loves us so much that He sent His only Son, Jesus, to take our sins upon Himself and die in our place. Jesus took the fall to pay the penalty for the sins of mankind. All who believe on Him will not perish but have eternal life. Dealing with forbidden fruit? Don't let it become a jam in your life. Give it to Jesus.

Tabernacle
FREE WILL BAPTIST CHURCH

WILL THE ROAD
YOU'RE ON GET TO
MY PLACE ... GOD

The way of life winds upward for the wise, that he may turn away from hell below.

—Proverbs 15:24

THE ROAD TO GOD

Will the road you are on lead you to God? Life is a two-direction journey. You are either on the road to God or the road away from God. The road to God is narrow and not so easy to follow. It takes humility, self-sacrifice, and surrender to find it and travel along it. The road away from God is quite wide and is easily found by our flesh. Unlike the narrow road, the wide road is crowded with travelers. These travelers are seeking pleasure and self-gratification. They seem not to know it, but the things they are chasing in this life are temporal things. They do not last, and so they do not satisfy or complete us.

> Enter by the narrow gate; for wide is the gate and broad is the way that leads to destruction, and there are many who go in by it. Because narrow is the gate and difficult is the way which leads to life, and there are few who find it.
>
> —Matthew 7:13–14

As with most things in this life, we have a choice. We can choose the road that leads to God and eternal life in Him, or we can reject that road for something else. Many, including me, have tried various roads and avenues in search of happiness, satisfaction, peace, etc. We all have a void in us that we want to fill or satisfy. There are times when the answers seem so close, but in the end, they elude us again and again. Solomon talks about it in the book of Ecclesiastes. In chapter 3 and verse 11, he states, "He [God] has made everything beautiful in its time. Also He has put eternity in their hearts, except that no one can find out the work that God does from beginning to end." That eternity placed in our hearts becomes a black hole, a bottomless pit that we try to fill with money, fame, pride, sex, human accomplishment, and many other temporal things the world has to offer.

Life is most certainly a journey, and like all journeys of any importance, it contains some bumps, turns, detours, and even potholes. These things actually serve to strengthen us if we are following God. Our scripture under the marquee sign (Proverbs 15:24) alludes to a journey that has some twists: "The way of life winds upward for the wise. . . ." It winds as you follow the narrow way, but it's going upward. When you are following the narrow road to God's place, there will be potholes, unexpected turns, and unplanned detours, as well as high points and low points. The thing that is constant is that it is not a totally smooth journey, but one of winding, which is how most of us live life as we follow God.

We know that we are living and growing in a lost world, a world fallen into sin and populated with many people who do not know God. Many of these people have all kinds of personal agendas to lift up and gratify self. It does not matter to many of them what they do that may hurt others or defame the name of the Lord. We who have come to know God and have received His grace are on a path that ends at His place. We are far from perfect ourselves, which is why our paths have some twists and turns, but if we keep our eyes on the Lord and continue to show others the way, our path will always wind upward. The apostle Paul said it so well:

> Always in every prayer of mine making request for you all with joy, for your fellowship in the gospel from the first day until now, being confident of this very thing, that He who has begun a good work in you will complete it until the day of Jesus Christ.
>
> —Philippians 1:6

Yet again, the winding is traveling upward for the wise. You may ask, "Who are the wise?" The wise are those who choose the path of Christ, the narrow road. Proverbs 1:7 informs us, "The fear of the Lord is the beginning of wisdom, but fools despise wisdom and instruction." Though life has its ups and downs, troubles and hurdles, for the wise it is always moving upward. The second part of the verse (Proverbs 15:24) says, "that he may turn away from hell below." There is an added dimension here. Not only does the life of the believer wind upward through life's different challenges, but the overriding reason for this upward movement is to not end up in hell below. The question that God is asking each one of us to take a hard and honest look at is this: *"Will the road you're on get you to My place?"*

Part 5

SIGNS OF OUR TIMES

And let us consider one another in order to stir up love and good works, not forsaking the assembling of ourselves together, as is the manner of some, but exhorting one another, and so much the more as you see the Day approaching.

—Hebrews 10:24–25

THE CHURCH IS A GIFT

The church is a gift instituted by God, but it is also an imperfect organism full of imperfect people. The real, and biblical, church is not buildings, stained glass, or steeples. The church is people, assembled together for the purpose of worshiping God and encouraging one another, especially as they see the day of Christ's return coming. The church is not made up of spiritual giants and pure, faultless supermen and superwomen of faith. The church has never been about people who have it all together. It's more of a spiritual hospital in many ways, filled with people who are at different stages in their spiritual journeys.

> The church is not a gallery for the exhibition of eminent Christians.
> —Henry Ward Beecher, nineteenth-century American preacher

The church was birthed in the book of Acts in chapter 2, but Jesus initially introduced the concept of the Christian church in the New Testament gospel of Matthew. In Matthew, chapter 16 and verse 18, Jesus said to Peter, "On this rock I will build My church, and the gates of Hades shall not prevail against it." To understand what He means by "on this rock," we have to back up to verse 13 and read through 17:

> When Jesus came into the region of Caesarea Philippi, He asked His disciples, saying, "Who do men say that I, the Son of Man, am?"
>
> So they said, "Some say John the Baptist, some Elijah, and others Jeremiah or one of the prophets."
>
> He said to them, "But who do you say that I am?"
>
> Simon Peter answered and said, "You are the Christ, the Son of the living God."
>
> Jesus answered and said to him, "Blessed are you, Simon Bar-Jonah, for flesh and blood has not revealed this to you, but My Father who is in heaven."

The question that Jesus asks ("Who do you say that I am?") cannot truly be answered by reading it in a book or learning it by rote in Sunday school. It must be revealed by God through the Holy Spirit. Peter's answer showed that for probably the first time, he really got it. He realized in his spirit exactly who Jesus was: the Son of the living God.

The "rock" that Jesus was talking about in verse 18 was Peter's revelation of who He (Jesus) was. Some people believe that because the name *Peter* means "little stone," or "rock," that Jesus was saying here that He was going to build His church upon Peter, a man. That is how the position of pope (leader of the Catholic Church) began. Some believe that Peter was the first pope in a long line of successors. Others, like me, believe the "rock" that Jesus talked about in verse 18 was Peter's revelation of exactly who Jesus was, and is.

It became more than lip service or a nice idea. It became real to Peter. That is the revelation that every believer must come to. On that *rock*, the church of Jesus Christ will be built, and the gates of Hades will not prevail against it. Jesus backed this thought up in verse 17 because He told Peter that the revelation of who He is came to him (Peter), not by flesh and blood, but by His Father in heaven.

I'm concerned that many of us who call ourselves Christian either have not had that epiphany or have somehow forgotten it. You may think that is something no believer could ever forget. I too once believed that Christians could not forget about their salvation in Christ, but look at 2 Peter 1, verses 5 through 7. Peter himself lists a number of godly virtues that we as Christians should be practicing and exhibiting on a regular basis: "for this very reason, giving all diligence, add to your faith virtue, to virtue knowledge, to knowledge self-control, to self-control perseverance, to perseverance godliness, to godliness brotherly kindness, and to brotherly kindness love." Then we get to verse 9, and he says, "For he who lacks these things is shortsighted, even to blindness, *and has forgotten that he was cleansed from his old sins* (emphasis added). We can forget the revelation of who Jesus is when we are not practicing these virtues. When we continue to assemble ourselves together, we remind and exhort one another to keep the revelation alive by practicing these biblical virtues daily.

Jesus initiated the gift (the beginning of the church), and in Acts chapter 2, it was birthed and began to grow rapidly. Because this gift from God grew so fast and was made up of finite, fallen human beings, problems began to slip into the church. Peter and others realized that to sustain this gift from God, they would have to become intentional in assembling it in a way that was God honoring. Jesus told them in Acts 1:8 that the Holy Spirit was there to empower them to live Christlike, and they had the Old Testament writings and the apostles' teaching to help guide them.

Psalms 127:1 says, "Unless the Lord builds the house, they labor in vain who build it." For us to be the church today, to be that gift of God, we cannot operate under a Lone Ranger mentality. The Bible says that wherever two or more are gathered in the name of Jesus, He will show up. To be the church of God, we have to be intentional about meeting together regularly to worship God corporately and encourage one another in the work of the Lord as we see the day of Christ approaching. When believers are practicing the virtues mentioned in 2 Peter 1:5–7, they grow individually in Christ. When they then assemble themselves together regularly, they become the church, and they become God's gift to the community.

Yes, the church is a gift from God, but a whole lot of assembly is required on our part.

Rejoice always, pray without ceasing, in everything give thanks; for this is the will of God in Christ Jesus for you.

—1 Thessalonians 5:16–18

CONSTANT RENEWAL

What is *constant renewal*? Does constant renewal mean that Christian men and women must get saved constantly? Second Corinthians 5:17 says, "Therefore, if anyone is in Christ, he is a new creation; old things have passed away; behold, all things have become new." Christians do not need to ask for salvation constantly, but as followers of Christ, we should be in a constant state of renewal. The life of a Christian is an ongoing walk of sanctification. That simply means we are always learning and maturing in our desire to be more like Jesus Christ.

> Through the LORD's mercies we are not consumed, because
> His compassions fail not. They are new every morning.
> —Lamentations 3:22–23

Wow! How cool is that? God knows that we are in a progressive walk toward Christlikeness, and He assures us His mercy and compassion are newly available to us every day. We live in a world where both evil and good reside. We know, even as Christians, that we fall short and are far from perfect. Our walk with the Lord is a constant learning experience. Some days are better than others, but as we continue to genuinely follow after Christ, His grace is sufficient for us.

We do not work for our salvation. Our salvation is assured through our confession of Christ, but we will work at sanctification all the days of our lives. Philippians 1:6 puts it like this: "Being confident of this very thing, that He who has begun a good work in you will complete it until the day of Jesus Christ."

Most of the directives and teachings in the Bible are not for a one-time experience. Biblical teachings speak of continually practicing and living out whatever truth the Bible is teaching. For example, in Matthew 7:7, Jesus teaches us, "Ask, and it will be given to you; seek, and you will find; knock, and it will be opened to you." The word *ask* here means to continually ask, *seek* means to continually seek, and *knock* in this context means to keep knocking.

Renewal is constant in the life of a Christian, and what opens our eyes and heart to this constant renewal is constant thanksgiving; that is, an attitude of gratitude. All through its pages, the Bible teaches the importance and benefits of thankfulness and gratitude. The Bible actually has much to say about the results of thankfulness in the life of a believer:

Be anxious for nothing, but in everything by prayer and supplication, with thanksgiving, let your requests be made known to God.

—Philippians 4:6–7

Continue earnestly in prayer, being vigilant in it with thanksgiving.

—Colossians 4:2

Many studies outside the Bible have also pointed to how constant thankfulness brings refreshing and renewal to folks who practice it. Gratitude, or thankfulness, has been said to mold and shape the entire Christian life. Martin Luther referred to gratitude as "the basic Christian attitude," and today it is still referred to as the heart of the gospel. According to Jonathan Edwards (1703–1758, theologian and revivalist), love, gratitude, and thankfulness toward God are among the signs of true religion. Edwards claimed that the "affection" of gratitude is one of the most accurate ways of finding the presence of God in a person's life. There certainly are other signs of God's hand on the life of a believer, but thankfulness is one of the quickest and easiest attributes to identify.

A large body of recent work has suggested that people who are generally grateful and thankful have higher levels of well-being. Grateful people are happier, less depressed, less stressed, and more satisfied with their lives and social relationships. These studies have shown that thankful, or grateful, people tend to have more control of their environment, personal growth, purpose in life, and self-acceptance. They have more positive ways of coping with the difficulties they experience in life and are more likely to seek support from other people.

For an experiment, if you don't do this already, purposely thank those around you at every encounter for the next thirty days. Thank a store clerk for handing you your change after a purchase. Thank a coworker for being there for you. Thank a stressed-out fast-food worker at the drive-through window; tell her you genuinely hope she has a great day, and so on. You get the idea. Thank people and bless them every chance you get. Be that little ray of sunshine in their long, arduous day. There is something about sincerely appreciating someone that can sometimes change their universe and perhaps inspire them to pass it on.

If you do this, it will change your life and everything around you. People will become friendlier and more helpful. Flowers will smell sweeter. The colors around you will be more vivid and alive. Difficult tasks will become character-building challenges. You will be amazed at all these outward attitudes and changes, but then hopefully realize there has actually been an inward change in you.

A man who has friends must himself be friendly, but there is a friend who sticks closer than a brother.

—Proverbs 18:24

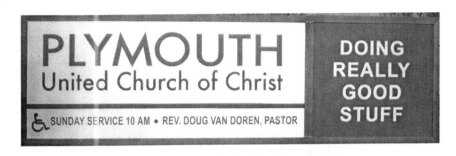

That word you know, which was proclaimed throughout all Judea, and began from Galilee after the baptism which John preached: how God anointed Jesus of Nazareth with the Holy Spirit and with power, who *went about doing good* and healing all who were oppressed by the devil, for God was with Him.

—Acts 10:37–38, emphasis added

DOING GOOD STUFF

When Jesus walked the earth two thousand years ago, He went about doing really good stuff wherever He went because God the Father was with Him. I am not talking about helping little old ladies across the street, volunteering at the local food pantry, or giving to foreign missions. Those are good things, but the really good stuff He did changed lives drastically. The good stuff He did changed the course of humanity. Of course, He was part of the Godhead, from where all good comes. James 1:17 says, "Every good gift comes down from the Father of lights."

From the very beginning, we see God creating things and pro-claiming that they are good: "Then God saw everything that He had made, and indeed it was very good. So the evening and the morning were the sixth day" (Genesis 1:31). Everything that God made was good until sin came into our world and began to eat away at the good. We were made to be and to do good. We were made to be the care-takers of God's good creation, but sin was introduced through Adam and Eve, which changed our world significantly.

There is still a portion of good in our world, but we also have much bad that seems to be progressing. One needs only to watch the evening news on any day to see all of the bad things happening around the globe. The Scriptures teach us that we have no goodness or righteousness of our own, but only through Jesus can we truly do the kind of good that will last and make a difference in our world.

When we come to know and accept Jesus as Lord, putting our faith in Him, our life on earth takes on new meaning. We become part of a worldwide movement that started with twelve men two thousand years ago. The mission of Christians is bringing the knowledge and goodness of Jesus to all. It gives us a greater purpose than just looking out for ourselves. Ephesians 2:10 puts it like this: "For we are His workmanship, created in Christ Jesus for good works, which God prepared beforehand that we should walk in them."

Primarily, we desire the rest of the world to know the Jesus of the Bible, but our righteousness in Christ also translates into acts of love and kindness to our neighbors far away and across the street. It is what drives missionaries to some of the darkest places on earth to model Jesus. They model Christlikeness, in part, by doing really good and practical stuff such as giving instructions in farming, building, first aid, and academic pursuits. This desire for good motivates us to give a helping hand to strangers and to cultivate a way of life that has us going the extra mile to be a blessing to all those around us. It is also what drives us to forgive, rather than retaliate against those who do us wrong. Romans 12:21 says, "Do not be overcome with evil, but overcome evil with good." We certainly are not perfect in doing these things, but true Christ-followers work at them regularly to be a blessing to all those around them, including Christ.

Learn to do good; seek justice, rebuke the oppressor; defend
the fatherless, plead for the widow. —Isaiah 1:17

161

Doing good stuff is far from just giving lip service. It has to do with living out our Christianity in the things we do. The Bible teaches that we are saved by faith in Christ alone, not by anything that we do. James helps to clarify this truth by teaching that although we are not saved by our works, our faith is evident to those around us by the good works we do. Our good deeds should always point to our Father in heaven. In Matthew 5:16, it is said like this: "Let your light so shine before men, that they may see your good works and glorify your Father in heaven."

This whole faith-versus-works argument has divided Christians and denominations for centuries. I happen to be of the school of thought that no one is good enough, based on their works, to make heaven their home. Jesus tells us in Mark 10:18, "No one is good but One, that is, God." But if there are no, or minimal, good works in your life, your Christianity may be more of a label than a lifestyle.

> How far that little candle throws his beams!
> So shines a good deed in a weary world.
> –William Shakespeare, *The Merchant of Venice*

When John the Baptist questioned whether Jesus was the Messiah, the Son of God, Jesus pointed to His works in the following story: One day Jesus' older cousin, John the Baptist, was imprisoned by King Herod for pointing out the sin in the king's life. While in prison, he sent his disciples to ask Jesus if He was the one they had been waiting for.

When the men came to Jesus, they said, "John the Baptist sent us to you to ask, 'Are you the one who is to come, or should we expect someone else?' " At that very time, Jesus cured many who had diseases, sicknesses, and evil spirits, and gave sight to many who were blind. So he replied to the messengers, "Go back and report to John what you have seen and heard: The blind receive sight, the lame walk, those who have leprosy are cleansed, the deaf hear, the dead are raised, and the good news is proclaimed to the poor."

—Luke 7:20–22

You can talk about your Christianity all day long, but it does not become real to people until it is modeled consistently in your life by the stuff you do. A kind, accepting, giving, forgiving, and helping attitude are all part of the really good stuff.

HE STANDS BEST
WHO
KNEELS MOST
WORSHIP 9:30-S.S. 11:00

And they continued steadfastly in the apostles' doctrine and fellowship, in the breaking of bread, and in prayers.
—Acts 2:42

HE STANDS BEST

Peter Marshall, born in Coatbridge, Scotland, in 1902, became pastor of the New York Avenue Presbyterian Church in Washington, DC, in 1937. He was appointed twice as US Senate chaplain, serving from January 4, 1947, until his sudden death just over two years later at forty-six years old. He once said, "If you don't stand for something, you'll fall for anything." The marquee sign here suggests that by making prayer a priority, we'll be able to stand in the diverse circumstances of life.

> If you don't stand for something, you'll fall for anything.
> —Peter Marshall

When the Christian church was getting started about two thousand years ago, the early converts devoted themselves to four major endeavors. These four are listed in Acts 2:42: "They devoted themselves to the apostles' teaching and to fellowship, to the breaking of bread and to prayer" (NIV).

1. Apostles' doctrine (common teaching)
2. Fellowship (community building)

3. Breaking of bread (communion)

4. Prayer (communication with God)

Because of their devotion to these four areas, the church added thousands to their number in a very short time. "Every day they continued to meet together in the temple courts. They broke bread in their homes and ate together with glad and sincere hearts, praising God and enjoying the favor of all the people. And the Lord added to their number daily those who were being saved." Acts 2:46-47 (NIV)

The beginning of the Christian church was an inspiring and exciting time for early Christians. Prayer was, and is still, an extremely important part of the church. In the beginning of my own ministry in the early nineties, I had the opportunity to hear one of our most revered, worldwide Christian statesmen teach on these scriptures in Grand Rapids, Michigan. His name was John Stott. I even managed to meet him and get a book signed. Stott died in 2011, but his teaching on the early church and prayer inspired me greatly. It caused me to devote myself to working in, for, and through the church of today to reach the lost, the last, and the least. I have learned firsthand that this work keeps you on your knees regularly.

I have been driven many times upon my knees by the overwhelming conviction that I had nowhere else to go. My own wisdom and that of all about me seemed insufficient for that day.

–Abraham Lincoln

Dr. Stott pastored All Saints Church in England for over thirty years, while taking a prominent role in drafting important evangelical documents like the 1974 Lausanne Covenant at the International Congress on World Evangelization held in Lausanne, Switzerland. This was attended by thousands of evangelical leaders from around the world. The creation of this covenant, outlining evangelical theology and reinforcing the need for social action, was a significant milestone in twentieth-century evangelicalism.

Stott wrote over fifty books, including *Basic Christianity*. Billy Graham called him "the most respected clergyman in the world." He was a man who taught the importance of prayer and who stood (and kneeled) for what he believed. Alister McGrath has suggested that the growth of postwar English evangelicalism is attributable more to John Stott than to any other person, and in 2005, *Time* magazine named him one of the one hundred most influential people in the world.

We can point to many Christian men and women leaders throughout history, and in the Bible, who spent much time on their knees. David Wilkerson, who founded the Teen Challenge program around 1960, was an ardent advocate of prayer. He explained once that in an eight-hour workday, he used to pray for the first hour and work the other seven, but he never seemed to get his work done. He said when he started to pray for the first three hours of the day, he seemed to always complete his work in the five hours remaining.

Over a century ago, a partially sighted African American minister, William J. Seymour, came to Los Angeles to share the message that the Holy Spirit still baptizes people with the evidence of speaking in tongues. His early efforts to preach the Pentecostal message were rejected. Church leaders were suspicious of his religious doctrine and his teachings, but he persevered and kept on praying.

He stood up for what he believed, regardless of ridicule and racial attacks. He was able to do this because of time spent on his knees.

At the time, the Los Angeles newspapers reported that contrary to rumors, there was no revival going on, just a bunch of little prayer groups around the city. Then, in April of 1906, a powerful outpouring of the Holy Spirit occurred within a small group of worshipers. There were physical and mental healings, speaking in unknown languages, and many other miraculous and inexplicable occurrences. The news spread, and soon thousands of people started coming from all over the world. Genuine revival broke out at the Apostolic Faith Mission on Azusa Street in Los Angeles as people came seeking to receive the Holy Spirit. It all started with people dedicated to prayer and willing to take a stand for what they believed.

Rejoice always, pray without ceasing, in everything give thanks; for this is the will of God in Christ Jesus for you.
– 1 Thessalonians 5:16-18

IF YOU CAN
READ THIS
SANDY ISNT HERE

Watch therefore, for you do not know what hour your Lord is coming. But know this, that if the master of the house had known what hour the thief would come, he would have watched and not allowed his house to be broken into. Therefore you also be ready, for the Son of Man is coming at an hour you do not expect.

—Matthew 24:42–44

SANDY'S NOT HERE YET

My wife, Sui, and I spent a week in Ocean City, Maryland, in mid-to-late October of 2012. It is widely known in the mid-Atlantic region of the United States as a summer destination for vacationers. The population was 7,102 at the 2010 census, although during summer weekends, the city hosts between 320,000 and 345,000 vacationers and up to 8 million visitors annually. During the summer, Ocean City becomes Maryland's second most populated town.[1]

One of the big tourist draws is the boardwalk, which is about forty city blocks long and borders the beach that separates the Atlantic Ocean from the city. It has all kinds of retail shops, eateries, and hotels along its length. When we were there, it was already a bit past the boardwalk season, but still warm and beautiful, especially along the ocean shore. Many of the shops were already closed for the winter, but again, it was sunny, beautiful, relaxing, and still filled with pedestrian tourists like us. The atmosphere gave no hint that within days all this would change quite dramatically.

Ocean City was in the path of what would soon become known as Hurricane Sandy. People were covering windows with plywood, buttoning up some areas and reinforcing others. The locals were getting prepared for a storm that promised to be one of the worst they had experienced, and we and other tourists were leaving town. We left for Michigan by car about twenty-four hours ahead of Sandy, and as we were leaving town, I took the photo of the restaurant marquee shown at the beginning of this writing: "If you can read this, Sandy isn't here."

Hurricane Sandy devastated portions of the Caribbean, the mid-Atlantic, and northeastern United States during late October 2012. There were also lesser impacts in the southeastern and midwestern states and eastern Canada. Sandy, classified as the eighteenth named storm and tenth hurricane of the 2012 Atlantic hurricane season, was a category 2 storm at its peak intensity here. While it was a category 1 storm off the coast of the northeastern United States, the storm became the largest Atlantic hurricane on record (as measured by diameter, with winds spanning 1,100 miles). Preliminary estimates of losses resulting from damage and business interruption in the US were estimated at $65 billion (2013 USD), which would make it the second-costliest Atlantic hurricane, behind only Hurricane Katrina. About 286 people were killed along the path of the storm in seven countries. In the United States, Hurricane Sandy affected twenty-four states, including the entire eastern seaboard from Florida to Maine and west across the Appalachian Mountains to Michigan and Wisconsin, with particularly severe damage in New Jersey and New York. Its storm surge hit New York City on October 29, flooding streets, tunnels, and subway lines as well as cutting power in and around the city.

I would like to have seen that restaurant marquee twenty-four to forty-eight hours after I took the photo. I'm sure it would have been dramatically different. Much of the boardwalk and other parts of Ocean City suffered damage from the storm, but the brunt of it hit just northeast of the city. Although meteorologists can give us some warning about coming storms today, we still seem to be unprepared for the extent of the damage they can do and the speed with which they lay destruction along their path. As of this writing, nearly two years since superstorm Sandy hit the eastern United States, there are still many families who lost everything and are basically homeless.

The scripture in Matthew 24:42–44 tells us that we will have no clear warning when the Lord comes back. Like a thief that comes in the night when we do not expect it is how the Lord will show up. So we are to live as though He could come at any moment. Matthew tells us that no man will know the exact time, but he does give us some helpful things to look for to let us know the end is close. In Matthew 24:6–8, the Bible says, "You will hear of wars and rumors of wars, but see to it that you are not alarmed. Such things must happen, but the end is still to come. Nation will rise against nation, and kingdom against kingdom. There will be famines and earthquakes in various places. All these are the beginning of birth pains."

This scripture is telling us that those signs mentioned are the beginning of the end times. If you follow the news, you know all these things are happening with frequency. Christians should have nothing to worry about if they have accepted the living Christ as Lord. When we sincerely receive Jesus as Lord, it means we want to be like Him. It's a lifetime journey as well as the journey of a lifetime. It's a process that Christians work at, and through, from the day of their salvation until they go to be with Jesus or Jesus returns.

I use Philippians 1:6 often because it is one of my life verses. It says it like this: "Being confident of this, that He who began a good work in you will carry it on to completion until the day of Christ Jesus." Christians are not perfect and without sin in their lives once they become true followers of Jesus. We still live in a fallen world where sin runs rampant, and we are in these fleshly bodies, which are tempted by sinful lusts. But we are forgiven because Jesus, who was without sin, paid the price for all of us who accept His lordship.

> Following Jesus is a lifetime journey,
> As well as the journey of a lifetime.

I read a caption somewhere that asked, "Will the last person leaving earth please turn the lights out?" One Bible interpretation teaches that Christians will be caught up in the sky to meet Jesus when He returns, and the world will face seven years of tribulation without the godly influences of Christians and the Holy Spirit. It will be a time of great suffering and devastation for those who are left on the earth. A marquee sign to "born again" Christians could read;

"If you can read this sign, Jesus hasn't come back yet."

WOLF LAKE
UNITED METHODIST CHURCH

TOUGH TIMES DONT LAST -
TOUGH PEOPLE DO

Not that I was ever in need, for I have learned how
to be content with whatever I have. I know how
to live on almost nothing or with everything. I
have learned the secret of living in every situation,
whether it is with a full stomach or empty, with
plenty or little. For I can do everything through
Christ, who gives me strength.
—Philippians 4:11–13, NLT

TOUGH TIMES, TOUGH PEOPLE

Tough times call for tough people. Right? Well, maybe, but I believe there is a particular quality that marks truly tough people. They understand where their strength comes from, just as the psalmist did in Psalm 121:1–2;

> I will lift up my eyes to the hills—
> From whence comes my help?
> My help *comes* from the LORD,
> Who made heaven and earth.

My help, or my strength, or my toughness, actually comes from the Lord Jesus Christ. That's who makes me tough enough to go through tough times. He gives me the strength to go through and the wisdom to know that difficult times have an end. Good times, hard times, exciting times, or boring times—they come and they go. But they do not go on forever. They are cyclical, like the yearly seasons. I know that some geographical locations do not have radically different seasons, but in Michigan, we have four dramatically defined seasons. We know that inevitably, they will come and they will go.

There is no question when the air temperature is ten degrees and there is three feet of white stuff on the ground that it is winter. When spring comes, the snow melts and new buds appear on the branches of trees that have been devoid of leaves for months. The air is pregnant with new life, great possibilities, expectations, and hope. Spring then gives way to summer with its hotter temperatures, more outside activities, and the cry of young men and women, "Surf's up, dude!" Well, they don't actually surf on the Great Lakes, that I know of, but you get the idea, fun in the sun. And then, of course, the air begins to cool, the wind picks up, and the leaves on the trees are transformed into the most beautiful hues of yellow, red, and brown before they fall to the ground. Again, there is no question (at least to native Michiganders) that fall, or autumn, is here.

The thing we know for certain about these seasons is that they come every year and they end every year. They have a beginning and an end. It seems that it would get boring and old to have one season that never changed. Life itself has many changes. We live in a world of great diversity, where times, situations, and circumstances are in a constant state of flux. In Michigan, we say, "If you don't like the current weather condition, wait five minutes; it'll change." So when troubles and tough times come your way, know that they have come to pass; they have an expiration date. The question I want to bring to your attention here is, what do you do while you are waiting for it to pass?

First of all, you cannot do it alone. This is a tough concept for some, particularly for men who are part of the baby-boomer generation and before. Many of us grew up hearing and watching stories of World War II heroes and tough cowboys who could grit their teeth, go it alone, keep their emotions from showing, and win the day.

They would rather die than show any kind of weakness, and when they did die, it was with their boots on. One has to ask the question, is that the right definition of what it means to be tough, or is it actually a facade built on a kind of weakness? Solomon said it well in Ecclesiastes 4:9–12:

> Two people are better off than one, for they can help each other succeed. If one person falls, the other can reach out and help. But someone who falls alone is in real trouble. Likewise, two people lying close together can keep each other warm. But how can one be warm alone? A person standing alone can be attacked and defeated, but two can stand back-to-back and conquer. Three are even better, for a triple-braided cord is not easily broken. (NLT)

We all need someone to help us shoulder the burdens we carry from day to day. We were not designed to go it alone. When God made Adam, he was alone; there was no other human for Adam to fellowship with. Then God said in Genesis 2:18, "It is not good for the man to be alone. I will make a helper who is just right for him" (NLT). The first source of help that Christians are to turn to is Jesus. It is He who gives us the strength we need to deal with the diversities of life.

> Take my yoke upon you. Let me teach you, because I am humble and gentle at heart, and you will find rest for your souls. For my yoke is easy to bear, and the burden I give you is light
> —Matthew 11:29–30, NLT

Second, as we are waiting for a particular season or trouble to pass, we have to realize that it is not to be passive waiting. There is much going on in our lives as we wait. Isaiah 40:29–31 puts it like this: "He gives power to the weak, and to those who have no might He increases strength. Even the youths shall faint and be weary, and the young men shall utterly fall, but those who wait on the LORD shall renew their strength; they shall mount up with wings like eagles, they shall run and not be weary, they shall walk and not faint." Our waiting on the Lord is not downtime. During those times, we should be productive, both in resting and building our spirit. We should be living life as usual—praying, reading and meditating on God's Word, helping others, and meeting with other believers for fellowship around our common purpose, which is to know Jesus and make Him known.

The Story of the Chinese Bamboo Tree

A man took the little seed of the Chinese bamboo tree, planted it, watered it, and fertilized it for a whole year, but nothing happened. The second year, he watered it and fertilized it, but nothing happened. The third year, he watered it and fertilized it, and again nothing happened. How discouraging this became! (He's already shown more patience than most of us.) The fourth year, he watered it and fertilized it, but still nothing happened.

After four years of waiting on and nurturing and watering, it was frustrating and seemed totally fruitless to the man. But if he were to continue to water and fertilize the seed, sometime during the fifth year, the Chinese bamboo tree would grow about ninety feet in six weeks. As the man who planted the seed waited to see growth, he watered and nurtured that seed. And even though he did not see the growth for a time, the roots were growing deeper and deeper as he waited and watered.

Life can be likened to the growing process of the Chinese bamboo tree. It is often discouraging. We keep doing things right, but nothing changes. Things may even get tougher. But if we are waiting on the Lord and believing we can do all things through Christ, we realize there will be seasons of waiting where we will continue to nurture, water, and build up our faith in God. And even though there is no discernible change that we can see in the natural, at some point we will experience great growth spurts in our Christian walk.

I am thankful that tough times don't last, but tough Jesus people do.

Doug and Sui Malear founded Hope Lighthouse Ministries in Muskegon Heights, Michigan, in 1996, just one year after they were married on April 1, 1995 (April 1 was Sui's idea).

Doug had lived homeless in the streets of Detroit, spent three years in Jackson Penitentiary, was addicted to heroin over a span of twenty years, and in 1986 identified his wife of ten years dead from a heroin overdose. It looked like the end. But God!

Sui endured years of abuse at the hand of her father, who died in prison just weeks after Sui visited and forgave him. But God!

Together, with dedicated volunteers, they minister in the Heights (Muskegon Heights) to the last, the lost and the least of these. The Heights is a three-square-mile city in west Michigan where high poverty, crime, and abuse plague the city. They feed hundreds of families every month, disciple men coming out of prison and off the streets, work at mentoring at-risk children who have no dad or too many dads coming and going, and operate church services and street outreaches.

Over the years, the family van has been stolen, a church van has been stolen, another church van has bullet holes, and they have replaced many windows in their storefront and houses. For every one kid who leaves the old life behind and genuinely accepts Christ, it seems like there are ten others who do not make it.

People ask the Malears why they minister in such a place; where teen age shootings are escalating, the school system is all but collapsing, families are fleeing the city and over six hundred houses in a population of ten thousand people are abandoned shells waiting to be torn down. They tell people that they opened their Bible one day to Psalms 148:1 and it says in part, "Praise Him in the heights." The Malears love and minister to the people of the Heights and the entire Muskegon area. Please keep them in your prayers.

Doug and Sui Malear Hope Lighthouse Ministries
2731 Peck Street Muskegon Heights, MI 49444

hopenthecity.org hopelighthouse@comcast.net

NOTES:

Title Page

1. Lyrics from the song, "Signs" recorded in 1971 by the Canadian group, Five Man Electrical Band http://en.wikipedia.org/wiki/Five_Man_Electrical_Band

Endorsement Page

1. New Vision Renewable Energy (NVRE). A non-profit, Christian Community Development organization in rural north central W. VA. NVRE engages and empowers youth across our nation in putting together portable, self-sustaining, solar energy devices that are relatively inexpensive and are saving lives around the world. For more information on how your youth, or youth group can get involved; www.NVRE.org

God Makes All Things New

1. Wikipedia contributors, "Louis E. Boone," *Wikipedia, The Free Encyclopedia,* http://en.wikipedia.org/w/index.php?title=Louis_E._Boone&oldid=560752750 (accessed July 2, 2014).

Men Die from Stubborness

1. "Hard to be Humble" hit song written & performed by Mac Davis in 1980 http://www.metrolyrics.com/its-hard-to-be-humble-lyrics-mac-davis

You have a Choice

1. Stephany Marston, Quote from "Right Choices" www.values.com/inspirational-**quote**-authors/1485-**Stephanie**-**Marston**

America's Joyous Future

Mondays and Thursdays: Drug and Alcohol Abuse

1. National Survey on Drug Use and Health (NSDUH) conducted by the Substance Abuse and Mental Health Services Administration and A major source of information on substance use, abuse, and dependence among Americans aged 12 and older. Facts and statistics on substance use in America from 2012, the most recent year for which NSDUH survey data have been analyzed. From www.drugabuse.gov/publications/drugfacts/nationwide-trends

Tuesdays: Spousal Abuse

2. Safe Horizon: "Moving victims of violence from crisis to confidence." From www.safehorizon.org/index/what-we-do-2/domestic-violence--abuse-53/domestic-violence-statistics--facts-195.html

Wednesdays: Eating Disorders

3. According to results published in the *Archives of General Psychiatry*.

Fridays: Teen (and Youth) Suicide

4. The Jason Foundation, Youth and teen statistics at <u>www.jasonfoundation.com/youth-suicide/facts-stats/</u>

Dusty Bibles

1. From Religious Tolerance web site at <u>www.religioustolerance.org/rel_coun2.htm</u>

Noah Was Prepared

1. Larry Norman, "I Wish We'd All Been Ready" written in 1969, lyrics from <u>http://www.onlyvisiting.com/gallery/lyrics/songs/ready/ready.html</u>

Keep It to Yourself

1. Using digital voice recorders over an eight-year period, researchers at the University of Arizona studied how many words hundreds of American and Mexican college students spoke over several days. The students carried the voice-activated recorders for almost all of their waking hours, on average about 17 hours a day. The study found that women spoke 16,215 words a day, while men spoke 15,669. Although women speak slightly more words than men, statistically, the difference is insignificant, according to Matthias R. Mehl, a psychology professor at the University of Arizona and the study's lead author. <u>http://abcnews.go.com/Technology/story?id=3348076</u>

Loose Talk – Free Speech

1. "Loose Lips Sink Ships," <u>www.phrases.org.uk/meanings/</u>

2. "Loose Lips Sink Ships" EyeWitness to History, www.eye-witnesstohistory.com (1997)

Famous Last Words
1. Frank Sinatra, "My Way" recorded and released by Frank Sinatra in 1969, lyrics found at http://www.metrolyrics.com/my-way-lyrics-frank-sinatra.html

Forbidden Fruit
1. America, "Back to the Garden" Lyrics found at http://www.sing365.com/music/lyric.nsf/Woodstock-lyrics-Crosby-Stills-Nash-Young

Sandy's Not Here Yet
1. http://en.wikipedia.org/wiki/Ocean_City,_Maryland (2014)

CPSIA information can be obtained
at www.ICGtesting.com
Printed in the USA
FFOW01n0726311017
41734FF